To Ann (without)

Are We Getting Through?

A Resource Book for Creative Communication

When Jesus spoke to the people, he told stories. Was Jesus unique in his approach? Should we do the same? How can Jesus' approach be applied today?

Are We Getting Through? considers both the How? and Why? of using stories to communicate more effectively. But it is more than just a resource book in creativity; at its heart is a touching story of how the discovery of creative ideas was crucial in the journey toward personal wholeness.

Included are over fifty stories, sketches and poems (with performance rights) interspersed with more than fifteen years' worth of principles and springboard ideas designed to help you become more creative in what you do.

Rob Lacey

Are We Getting Through?

A Resource Book for Creative Communication

Silver Fish
publishing

British Library Cataloguing in Publication Data
A record for this book is available from the British Library

ISBN 1 902134 11 7

Printed and bound in Great Britain by
Cox & Wyman, Reading, Berks

Silver Fish Publishing is a division of
Silver Fish Creative Marketing Ltd,
37 Pottery Lane, Holland Park,
London W11 4LY

For Sandra, my wife and best friend

Rob Lacey is a gifted communicator. He understands his audience and finds wonderfully creative ways of getting through to them. He knows how to teach others to do the same. The ideas, principles and arguments of this book deserve careful consideration — they could transform both you and your evangelism.
Phil Wall, national evangelist, Salvation Army

This is not a drama book! This is a book about communication. Anyone serious about improving their communication skills would benefit from getting to grips with this book.
Jeff Lucas, vice president, Evangelical Alliance

Rob Lacey's work is always enjoyable and highly original. This book is no exception. I believe it will give you many new ideas, and improve your understanding of how to connect with people more effectively.
Rob Frost, Methodist National Evangelist

Rob Lacey is one of the most effective communicators I have come across. Often the people who should write the How To books almost never do. I am delighted that Rob has. He does not write because "he has to say something", but because he has something to say. Communicators, buy this book!
J John, speaker

This book is based on the fact that we are all reflections of a creator God. It shows, in practical and inspirational ways, how we can maximise this God-given creativity in worship and communication with others.
Faith Forster, Ichthus Christian Fellowship

Acknowledgments

Thanks to...
(cast in order of appearance)

Father God,
who first thought of me and set out his plans for me.

My parents,
*whose combination of fun and depth of feeling have been such a secure
foundation throughout.*

Dave Colman,
who first inspired me in creativity and faith.

All those who were part of Trapdoor Theatre Company from '84 to '91.

Gareth Knowles,
a friend through fun and fear — so much more than a fine set designer.

Paul Francis and all at Going Public Trust,
who've been a huge support since the Trapdoor slammed shut.

Sandra,
my wife, partner, colleague and best friend.

Brian Spense,
*whose company Ethical Financial have kept me on the road by
sponsoring a car.*

Phil and Julie Stokes, Richard and Caro Swan
*at Ichthus Church, Camberwell, for their prayers, friendship and
practical support.*

Those who read and responded to earlier drafts of this book:
Peter Lacey, Anthony Millin, Paul Francis, Sarah Fordham, Mike
Bernardin, Faith Forster and Nick Pollard.

Contents

Introducing The Plot 11

Creative Communication 17
Why do we need creative communication? 19
Who can be creative? 22
How can we be more creative? 25
Directions 25
Who's To Blame? 26
All The Eights, Eighty Eight 32
All The Eights, Eighty Eight (part two) 33
All The Eights, Eighty Eight (part three) 34
All The Eights, Eighty Eight (part four) 34
Introducing the Writes of Passage 37

The Bible as Source 39
Good News 42
Scramble Scramble 44
Juggling Jack 48
I Was Fine 51
Why? 53
The Ten Commandments 59
The Perfect Sketch 60
The Sower 61
The Flowers Told On Me 64
Psalm Twenty Three And A Half 65
The Prodigal Son 67
Monologues From The Prodigal 70
Conclusion 71

Our Own Stories as Source 77
Non-Stop World 80
Blind Man's Bluff 81
Do I Climb? 82
Joint Cell 85
Job Satisfaction 87

No One Knows Now 89

Making Bad Things Go Away 91

Insanity 92

Counting Backwards From Ten 93

Concentration Span 95

Harness The Darkness 96

Your Woodginess 98

Your Woundedness 98

Some Days 99

Both Ways (The Poem) 100

Both Ways (The Sketch) 101

Both Ways (The Song) 103

People Like Me 104

The Wood Chopper 105

Conclusion 107

Other People's Stories As Source 111

I'm A Skoda 115

In An Hour 116

How Do I Pray? 118

Musicians Cheat! 119

Mr Kalashnikov 120

God Is... 121

Happy Families 122

Addicted 128

Saying "No" To Drugs 129

Compassion Fatigue 132

Death By Soap 136

I've Got A Friend 141

More Than An Orphan 142

Our Father 143

Lord, Take Control 145

Paradise Crushed 146

Justice, He Knows How It Goes 146

Conclusion 151

The View From This Point Of The Journey 153

The Salesman 158

Not By... 171

Epilogue 173

Lip Reading 173

Introducing
The Plot

Introducing The Plot

The beginning

Like all good stories, this book begins with setting the scene and establishing the challenge. The scene is set in a media-dominated culture, where stories are the language of the people and the Church is trying to communicate effectively. The questions are posed: Are we getting through? Are we speaking a language that people understand? Would we benefit from being more creative in our communication? If so, how can this happen?

Collecting tools for the journey

The challenge of today raises more questions. Is creative communication only for certain types of people? Can we all be creative? How can we be more creative? We'll look at the conditions in which creativity is likely to flourish, where to look for creative ideas and how we can use the Six Questions of Craft — Who? Where? What? When? How? and Why? — to develop these ideas further.

The middle

In the main section of the book we'll move onto the "Writes of Passage" — the important moments, ideas and events that brought me to writing this book. This includes specific material which you are free to use, but more importantly also includes reflections on the process behind the ideas; principles and springboard suggestions designed to stimulate you toward producing your own material.

The Writes of Passage have been structured in response to the frequently asked question: "Where do ideas come from?" The three sections are organised according to where the idea originated, its source:

1 The Bible
2 Our own stories
3 Other peoples' stories.

Each of these sections is set out in chronological order allowing you to see the progression of ideas toward my three current shows. You'll also notice that, as with any good story, there is a definite development in the character himself (*ie*, me) as the story unfolds.

The main emphasis throughout is on our communication, *ie* our "outreach", which is where the journey toward understanding creativity began for me; with the desire to be effective in outreach. But I couldn't have known how much "inreach" (reflection and self awareness) and "upreach" (prayer and worship) would be needed to keep me moving on toward effective outreach. Creativity rarely leaves the creator unchanged. The situations and challenges along the way have certainly changed me. I'm not the same person at the end as I was at the beginning. Creativity is like that.

More to the point, God is like that — he's not only concerned with how we fulfil our role in the kingdom, he's also very concerned with our personal development. I'm very grateful to God for the way he has repeatedly spoken to me through what I've created. Increasingly being creative has become not just something I use in order to do my job better, but something which has helped make me a fuller, more whole person. It's important that we don't separate our work from who we are. Thus the three areas of inreach, upreach and outreach must go hand in hand in hand:

- Too much inreach and not enough upreach can lead to unhealthy introspection;
- Too much upreach and not enough outreach can isolate us from people;
- Too much outreach and not enough inreach can make us too simplistic in our communication.

We need to find a balance. Allow each area to feed the others. Consequently, I've not only included material which can be used in outreach, I've also included more reflective and worshipful material. Communication is about being believable, about being authentic and having something about us that grabs the attention (ideally the Spirit of God). That is why the people listened so avidly to Jesus; it wasn't just that he told good stories, there was something captivating about who he was. May God teach us not only how to communicate, may he also change us so that he can communicate powerfully through us. All the clever creative techniques in the world won't have the desired impact unless God is working on us, and we are moving towards who and where he wants us to be.

The principles and practical ideas for increasing our creativity in our communication are drawn from the arena of creative writing and dramatic performance, since this has been my job for the last twelve years (with Trapdoor Theatre Company and subsequently as a solo writer and performer). I am convinced that the principles of creative writing and performance are highly relevant and easily applicable to most other styles of communication. I'm sure you won't have to be too creative to apply these ideas to what you do!

The end

The book ends with a resolution — to be more like Jesus. In the concluding chapter we'll consider the fact that when Jesus spoke to the general public he primarily told stories and asked questions. We'll look at what other people have said about Jesus' approach, and ways in which we can apply Jesus' approach to draw people into exploring the Christian gospel for themselves. We'll do this by again asking the Six Questions of Craft:

Who are we communicating with?
> Fellow fallen people who still retain some of the image of God and therefore deserve our respect.

Where are we communicating?
> On common ground, moving away from an "us and them" situation toward non-confrontational interaction.

What should we use to communicate?
> What Jesus used: stories and questions.

When are we communicating?
> In a Post-modern era, which allows us to tell stories, but struggles with claims to having absolute truth.

How should we communicate?
> Like Jesus did, by telling stories and asking questions, rather than giving people more than they were ready for.

Why should we tell stories and ask questions?
> Because this decreases our ability to control the situation, and gives more space for God to work.

A series of questions are provided for you to reflect on what God may be saying to you about the issues of creative communication raised in this book. Just because we have a beginning, a middle and an end doesn't mean that you have to read the book in that order. You may choose to move straight to the last chapter, if you want to find out how it ends and then return to the middle section to see how I got to this point. It's your choice.

Creative Communication

Creative Communication

Why do we need creative communication?

> He went to his first opera that night; to his surprise it was in Italian and since he understood none of it, he took the whole performance to be a kind of religious service.
>
> John Irving; *The World According To Garp*

How are we going to engage with people if we're not talking the same language? The need for creative communication is not just a nice idea or an indulgence. We have a crucial, life changing message to get across, and we need to be sure we're speaking the same language. But the language of our culture is changing. Are we aware of this? If so, have we fully thought through how this affects our methods of communication? If not, we'll be making very little sense to the people we passionately want to reach.

It's a huge challenge. If the language of society is changing, we'll have to learn this new language if we're going to get through and genuinely connect with people. We British are notoriously lazy when it comes to learning other languages. There's a lot of truth in the stereotypical image of British tourists expecting foreigners to understand them by simply speaking English slower and louder. Occasionally we're really considerate and throw in a couple of phrases dredged up from our schooldays. But basically there's no way we're going to learn a new language, especially because we know we don't have to since they all speak such good English. We're spoilt. They rely on our custom and so they work hard at our language and harder still at remaining polite!

As tourists, of course, we're probably only abroad for two weeks every other year. So our reticence to learn a new language is understandable. But what if it's fifty-two weeks of the year? What if we're living permanently in a culture that speaks a different language? Well, we are! The changes that have occurred over the last thirty or forty years have radically changed the culture we're living in. Further, because these changes have been gradual we've not realised that some of the communication styles that worked in the past are now largely a foreign language to people of today's generation.

We've learned these painful lessons in the past. In former colonial days, when we sent out missionaries we made the mistake of expecting the natives to change and become "civilised" (or rather Westernised) like us. Today we are far more thorough; we train our missionaries to speak the language and learn the culture of the people they're hoping to reach. But are we in danger of repeating the mistakes of the nineteenth century in our own country? Can we really expect people to listen to our ideas in a language that is alien to them? The call is to be humble enough to learn the language of our culture — to find relevant ways of communicating with the people in the media-dominated world of today.

This is difficult. The ground has shifted under our feet. There are very few places today where you'll hear the vocabulary of logical, reasoned argument; one is the university lecture hall, another is church. Even party political broadcasts have woken up to the fact that people won't listen to even a ten minute talk. As Steve Chalke has said:

> Story is the way the majority of people learn their values. If you put a discussion about euthanasia on *Panorama* the vast majority turn off mentally, if not physically. But if you put it in the plot of *EastEnders*, everybody's talking about it the next day.
>
> Steve Chalke, Oasis Trust

Listening to a rational, reasoned argument is alien to the way the majority of people in today's culture receive information. Many people today form their values and ideas from the characters and plot lines of soaps and films. It's all very well wishing this wasn't true, or digging our heels in and trying to make them concentrate harder. But is it going to work?

In the past our society was dominated by the influence of the Enlightenment, which emphasised scientific thought over mystery and emotion. This era was summed up by Descartes' famous quote: "I think therefore I am." This emphasis on the rational led to the marginalisation of subjective experience in preference to objective facts. But society is going through huge changes. To use the jargon, we have experienced a paradigm shift from Modernism into Post-modernism. To avoid the jargon, people today seem more interested in experience than theory, in peoples' stories rather than peoples' ideas. Surely, this is bound to demand a reassessment of our communication methods.

The Enlightenment championed the left half of the brain — the rational, logical part of us. The recent ground shift gives more freedom to the expression of the other half of the brain — the right half, which deals in pictures, emotions and feelings. God, of course, is fully capable of communicating to people whichever side of the brain they use — he made both halves! But he also chooses to use us. He calls us to be his mouthpiece, and we need to consider carefully how we fulfil this responsibility. Roy Clements has said:

> Post-modernists are reacting against rationalism and wishing to affirm the value of intuitive and subjective modes of human awareness. Arguably such a corrective reaction was necessary… [People] are suspicious of scientific materialism and open once again to spirituality.
>
> But they demand subjective involvement with that spirituality rather than mere cerebral information about it. Expository preachers cannot speak with relevance to a Post-modern audience unless they take this new situation to heart… In addition to informing the mind, God seeks to address the will and the feelings… Good exposition invites the listener to feel with the text as well as to think about it. The leaders of the evangelical revival in the eighteenth century broke away from arid and cerebral dissertations on divinity in order to preach to the heart. In a Post-modern culture we neglect that subjective dimension at our peril.

So please don't misunderstand me, this is not a book about "using drama more". Rather, this book is about how the church communicates. It's about all types of communicators having the courage and humility to reassess our approach in the light of our changing culture and being willing to learn new languages if necessary. Being a drama practitioner, of course I believe passionately in drama and in the principles of storytelling. I believe these principles are becoming more and more important in our media-dominated society. My hope is that my reflections will stimulate you in your journey toward effective communication.

Rob Parsons says:

> I have spent quite a lot of my Christian ministry in Bible
> teaching and especially apologetics, but it struck me some years
> ago that to convey a truth is not enough; we need to apply
> truth to people's lives to make it relevant to their situation.
> Jesus did this by using word pictures and stories which act as
> "windows on the soul" and which the Holy Spirit can use to
> make truth live.
>
> > Rob Parsons, Executive Director of Care for the Family

My hope is that this book will contribute something toward showing
both why we need to do this, and how it can be done.

Who can be creative?

> Just imagine for a moment, that we were made by a creative God. More
> than that, imagine that this creative God put his own character into us,
> because he wanted us to be creative too. Imagine that he longed for us
> to have a tiny glimpse of the thrill he had when he made the whole
> world out of nothing. Imagine he put his Spirit inside us to free us,
> inspire us and enable us to become all we can be. Then imagine his
> heart soaring every time we create something because we're being like
> him.
>
> What if all this were true? But then, imagine how he would feel if
> his people continually held back from enjoying their creativity because
> they were too busy, too frightened, or just plain lazy. Imagine that when
> they did create, they reigned in the leaping of their hearts and forced
> themselves to appear humble, refusing to enjoy what they'd made, and
> certainly not admitting that "it was good." How would God feel, if all
> this were true?
>
> Finally, imagine that this wonderful God didn't put false guilt on
> people. Imagine that he understood our weaknesses and our fears and
> wanted to draw us slowly into all the good things he has for us. Just
> imagine! Wouldn't it be great to have a God like that?

Sometimes we act as if we aren't made in the image of a creative God.
But surely this is a central part of our faith. We are creative! Every
time we have an idea, tell a story, plan a talk, answer a question,
adapt to a situation — we're being creative. But as with any loving
father, God says "Great, I'm proud of you, well done. Now what else

do you think you could do?" He wants us to progress.

My hope is that some of the ideas in this book will stimulate you towards where God wants you to be with your communication. But it's a difficult line to tread. My concern is that books of resource material can, ironically, stop some people from exploring their own creativity. The combination of a busy lifestyle, an instant-solution culture and a "handy scripts" book may actually distract people from discovering their own creative talents. Why produce your own talks or stories or poems or sketches when you can get ready-made ones from a book?

When I started using my creativity in outreach I didn't know there were any script books. I just busked my way through with a group of friends. Would we still have come up with our own ideas if we'd known we could have just lifted scripts out of a book? Who knows. That's not to say that there's nothing creative in adapting a story or script from the page to the pulpit or stage; nor is it to say that because we're all creative, that we are all able to write scripts. Creativity takes many forms and the nature of the Body of Christ is that we're all meant to be creative in what we're called to be doing. However, numerous creative workshops have convinced me that people are much more capable in this area than they often assume.

My other concern is that by using other people's material, you might be kept from finding your own voice. The material in most resource books has usually been written for specific individuals. In one sense this is good writing — the scripts are tailor-made for the skills and style of those who are to bring them alive. But when these scripts are published and other people take on the material, it can feel like having to wear a costume that doesn't quite fit. Sadly, people usually assume that it's a lack of faith on their part (not "in their part" obviously, since it was written by a professional!) and so they struggle on, and try to make it fit.

Take the story of David and Goliath: as soon as David volunteered to "go out there", for some reason everyone backstage assumed he would wear Saul's armour. There was huge pressure on him to do so. And he tried. But fortunately he had the presence of mind to realise that it just wasn't him. Instead he went out there as himself, with the skills he had, aware of his own vulnerability and his reliance on God's protection. And I think you'll agree, he turned in a pretty good performance!

The story wouldn't quite have the same feel to it if David had carried on, struggling to make Saul's armour fit, or rather, to make himself fit Saul's armour. He could have rehearsed and rehearsed, trying his hardest to be natural while wearing it. But ultimately it wouldn't have worked. Pretty soon he would've died at the hands of Goliath, in front of an audience of jeering Philistines.

Clearly, this issue relates to most styles of communication. There's no way of knowing how influenced we have been by those who have inspired us. But have we ever asked what makes them such effective communicators? Isn't it the very fact that they've found their *own* voice? No wonder it all seems to flow so naturally — it's the real them! I'm sure that God wants us to learn from others, but at the right time he wants us to leave these influences behind us and become ourselves — find our own voice.

My passion is that more and more people will take risks and do their own thing; reaching inwards and upwards rather than shelf-wards for that creative idea, that people would say what God has given them to say and say it in a way that honours how he's made them. Surely this will grab peoples' attention, since we're all on the alert for something that rings true. Not only will it have authenticity, but when we risk offering something genuinely authentic, we're on the edge of ourselves and need supernatural help — the Holy Spirit really can turn up.

So I've included material which you're welcome to use, but my hope is that by including observations and principles of how these ideas happened, you'll be inspired to produce your own. In this way, my aim is to apply the principle of "give a man a fish, you feed him for a day; teach a man to fish, he can feed himself for life." But in this case my role is not even to give you a fishing rod — you already have all you need since you are made in the image of a creative God. But hopefully this book will help you realise you're already using it, and perhaps how you can use it more effectively.

If you are creative, and if you believe that God is interested in your progress, and that he'll catch you if you fall, then go for it. Take that next step and move even closer to where he wants you to be.

Employing the gifts and abilities he's entrusted to us, which we've recognised, released for his use, and repeatedly honed, Christ will inspire whatever form of creativity he has given us; be it the gift of music, lyricism, poetry, drama, humour, pathos, mime, dance, performance, tapestry, painting, sculpture, sketching, recitation, acting, filming, production, direction, conducting, writing, singing, carpentry or design, in order to tell a story. A story in which he has the pre-eminence, in which one aspect of his Truth is hidden, to be discovered by those who want to understand as the Holy Spirit reveals it to them.

Gordon Bailey, Schools Outreach Trust

Creativity isn't only for certain types of people. It's also for the not-so-certain types of people.

How can we be more creative?

It's all very well saying "we're all creative", but something a little more practical would help! How do we get there? How can we find our creativity? It's easy! Just follow these simple directions:

Directions

Turn left after the empty crisp packet, right after the coke can on the wall and straight on past the bloke in trainers smoking a fag. As soon as you see a red car going the other way, take a sharp right at the next green hedge. Then you'll see some dog doo-doo on the pavement – you can't miss it, keep going down there, 'til you pass three parked cars. Just after the third car turn right and you'll go into a street with houses on it. Left at the next sparrow, left again at the shopping trolley, keep going down there for about three verses of Cwm by yah my Lord, and you'll get to a car with a three legged cat on the bonnet – I think it answers to the name of Fuzzy, if that helps. You'll find it in the house with the seagull on the roof and a black plastic dustbin bag outside. At least, that's the way I went when I found it.

In the rest of this book I've chosen to outline my journey toward more creative communication not because I believe everyone should travel the same way, or even get to the same point — that would be absurd (as the piece above shows). Rather, I've outlined the process as a way of discussing the issues, admitting the struggles and sharing the excitements of new discoveries that were all part of the journey. Along the way there will be practical reflections, principles and springboard ideas designed to stimulate you as you move forward in your communication skills.

But before we launch into the journey, let's establish some foundations. Where do ideas come from? How do they happen? Do dynamic, creative ideas only happen if you're brilliant or lucky or inspired by God? Or is it possible to create conditions in which ideas are more likely to flourish? If creative ideas are seeds, and we are the soil, what can be done to make and keep our soil fertile? As we've just seen, we are all intended to be fertile, but sometimes the climate in which we find ourselves has drained us of that fruitfulness. How do we get the life back into our soil so that ideas can grow again?

We will all create in unique ways and different styles, but for most creative acts the principles are the same. So let's look at a couple of poems, and draw out some principles. The first poem is deliberately non-Christian in content, so that we focus purely on the creative process.

Who's To Blame?
(September 1992)

He picks his toenails by the telly when he's sitting far too close
And the crumbs get scattered as he chomps his toast
Cuts the bread on the breadboard that is kept for show
He should know. He should know.

He always eats his pudding but he leaves his greens
Has a skill for playing football in his brand new jeans
Then he sits on the grass when he knows that it's damp
And the collywobbles come, and he's doubled up with cramp.

He should know. He should know.
'Cos his mum tells him so:
"Every time you play with it is one less time before it breaks,
It'll end in tears, stop showing off
Just settle down, for all our sakes."
But who's to blame at the end of the day?
When he won't pack his action men away

He lets his games kit fester in his locker for a week
Never hits the target when he takes a leak
Then fails to inform when the loo roll ends
Never waits 'til six to phone his friends.
He should know. He should know.

Throws the keys of the car when there might be a drain
Forgets to close the sunroof when they've forecast rain

Leaves the top off the toothpaste and the tap to drip
Tightens up the Branston with his iron grip.

He should know. He should know.
'Cos his mum tells him so:
"Every time you play with it is one less time before it breaks,
It'll end in tears, stop showing off
Just settle down, for all our sakes."
But who's to blame at the end of the day?
Is his mum to blame at the end of the day?
When he won't pack his action men away.

Stirs the non-stick pan with the metal spoon
Leaves his mugs piled up in his bomb-site of a room
Leaves the wrong lights on and the right lights off
Never covers his mouth when about to cough
Leaves butter in the sun when the weather's hot
Leaves homework undone, leaves leaves to rot
Dunks his digestives, leaves stubble round the sink
Burps in public, blows bubbles in his drink
Speaks with his mouthful, licks the curd off his knife
— No! *Lemon curd.* — Will he ever find a wife?

But who's to blame at the end of the day?
Is his mum to blame at the end of the day?
Is it Mrs Hussein who must take the blame?
When he won't pack his action men away
Who's to blame when Saddam says:
"No I won't pack my action men away,
I won't pack my action men away, so *ner!*"

There are several key principles brought out by how this poem
happened:

Firstly, start where you are

> A tourist asks for directions. The reply: "You want to get
> where? Oh you can't get there from here!"

If someone had asked me to produce a three minute comic poem,
suitable for a family audience, on the theme of tyranny, I would've

frozen — and nothing grows in frozen soil. Where would I have started? But turn this on its head — start where you are with a seed idea, let it grow naturally and you could end up anywhere! There are no limits.

But isn't that part of the problem? Many of us don't want to end up just anywhere. We want to end up somewhere specific — at a point where we can make a Telling Spiritual Point. All too often there are limits, strict, self imposed limits, which stem from a false view of God's attitude to creativity. God doesn't want us to be creative so we can market him better. God wants us to be creative because that's how he made us. Naturally some of our Christian worldview will come through in what we create, but that's not why we should be creative.

God did not inscribe Bible texts into tree trunks, nor did he only create fish-shaped land masses! But then he also didn't have to cope with all the baggage of trying to decide what was spiritual (and therefore worthwhile) and what was secular (and therefore to be avoided). He just loved making things! Sometimes he even made things for no apparent reason — why do men have nipples?

All too often our creativity is called on to produce something for a specific project. Sometimes this is how it has to be. But why not turn this around? Why not start where we are, with what we know, with the skills we have, with the stories that have happened to us. Not only will the ideas flow, but they'll also be more likely to ring true.

People are looking for integrity. They respond much more readily to honesty and vulnerability than to cold, disembodied truth. By making it a general principle that we'll start where we are and only say what we know, we'll avoid the pitfalls of trying to shoe-horn spiritual truths into every idea we have. Obviously there's nothing wrong with seeing spiritual parallels in everyday images, ideas and situations. The problems arise if we force them to fit — just try and get a spiritual message into the Saddam Hussein poem and you'll probably see what I mean!

Secondly, playfulness

"Rob, mess about more!"

Desmond Jones, mime tutor

As with many ideas, the Saddam Hussein poem happened when I was messing about. A friend and I were comparing notes on the things our mothers used to say (and sadly, still do). We had a good chortle, then we asked "What would happen if other people had mums like this?" and then "What if even fearful tyrants had mums like this?" and then "What if Saddam Hussein had a mum like this?" Don't ask me why. We just did. Which raises the question: What would happen if we asked "What would happen if...?" more often?

You'll find this hard to believe, but when I was growing up there were occasions when we four children got a little excited and rowdy. Inevitably a drink would be spilt or a toe would be stubbed, and my mum would deliver the line: "Now that wouldn't have happened if you'd not been messing about" (one of the many lines that didn't quite make it into the poem). This of course is true. But it's also true that electricity wouldn't have happened if Edison hadn't been messing about. History tells us that Thomas Edison was taking an afternoon off, flying his kite on the common when lightning struck. In that moment, so the story goes, the idea for electricity also struck. This must have been the very first cartoon-style "lightbulb above the head" moment, and like the Saddam poem, it would not have happened if he'd not been messing about.

At the end of my first term at Mime and Physical Theatre School, my tutor took me to one side and said "Rob, mess about more". No teacher had ever said such a thing to me (for good reason), but he realised that in my keenness to learn I was trying too hard. So I was blocking the creativity that comes from spontaneity and playfulness. This is especially the case if, as it was for me, we want to use our creativity to communicate our faith. Just because we're dealing in life-changing subjects is no reason to become sombre and intense. We can end up simply trying too hard. My tutor's quiet word served to release the tension and the next two terms were much more productive, and far more fun.

And let's not pretend it isn't fun. When children make something that excites them, there's no stopping them from celebrating their achievements. But of course we're much more sophisticated than that, aren't we? Shame! Why aren't we more like our Father? I have a feeling that, on the evening of the sixth day of creation God did not sit down and calmly say "It is very good". It strikes me as much more likely that he leapt around the heavens unable to control his excitement at the incredible things he'd just made.

God wants us to celebrate our creativity, to enjoy being like him, and not be too "grown up" about it. Are we so scared that people might think we're proud that we suppress the thrill of having made something? Children aren't proud, they just celebrate. Who was it that said: "Unless you change and become like little children, you cannot enter the kingdom of heaven"?

It makes me wonder whether the reason children cuddle adults is because they know we're not allowed to play?

Thirdly, time

> During times of crisis, and this is one, we desperately need reflection and clarity of vision to act with presence of mind. Let us therefore encourage one another to keep still long enough... to return to our own still centre, to be inspired and rekindle our love.
>
> Alida Gersie, *Earthtales*

Another crucial factor in this poem happening was that I had some spare time to play with the idea. The initial idea was sparked by "where I was" and by playfulness, but would I have spent all that time playing if I'd been stressed by deadlines and urgent tasks? Probably not. After all, the idea might have amounted to nothing, and then I'd be even more stressed having wasted my time. This then becomes a lifestyle issue: how do we manage our time? Do we see creativity as something important enough to set aside quality time? If so, are we ruled by the urgent or by the important?

Ideas are shy. They rarely wave their arms about to attract our attention. They sit calmly in quiet places and wait for us to turn off the television. Then, sometimes, they nudge us and ask if we're coming out to play. Ideas don't always happen when we take time to reflect, but they are much more common in quiet moments than when we're chasing our tails. Maybe this is why so many people get ideas last thing at night, when they're trying to get off to sleep — because, with our busy lifestyles, this is one of the rare times we stop and think.

It does take time. What's more, not all of what we produce will be useful in outreach. For every ten ideas I have, maybe five will be completed and perhaps only two will be of use. Of course we can justify this by considering it as time spent developing our writing skills so that future ideas will communicate the Gospel more effectively. Or we can say that the two ideas deemed to be of use are worth the time spent on the eight ideas deemed to be useless. But do we have to justify it? Why do we have to justify being more like our Father?

Fourthly, perseverance

A Mars a day helps you work, rest and play.

Some rich advertising executive

This is the third part of the triangle of "work, rest and play", and the three are very much interlinked. You tend to work harder when you're playing, play can be as good as a rest, you rest better after hard work, you work harder after a good rest, and so on. Most of the time I enjoyed putting this poem together, but there were moments when I had a block, when a rhyme wouldn't happen, or when I'd read the line too many times for it to be funny anymore. In these moments I just had to work on it. No way round it. I just had to put in the ninety-nine per cent perspiration that generally accompanies the one per cent inspiration. Sorry!

Fifthly, freedom to fail

There is hope in honest error. But none in the icy perfections of the mere stylist.

Charles Rennie Mackintosh, architect

This is probably one of the most important principles. If we're not free to fail we'll never try anything unless we're absolutely sure it'll work — and how can we be sure it'll work until we've tried it? This can become a vicious circle which keeps us locked inside our safe areas and never allows us to push back the boundaries.

If only we could grab hold of the fact that our value doesn't come from what we do, but rather from who we are. This would allow us so much more freedom to try things, to take risks and to develop our talents. Almost certainly we'd fail at times, ideas wouldn't come, things wouldn't work out, people wouldn't get it. But this shouldn't affect how we feel about ourselves and so we'd keep on trying. We'd even get to learn from our mistakes. All because our security was in who we are, not in what we do.

When I put this poem together I hadn't grasped this. To be honest, I wasn't even aware that my value *could* be in who I was, not in what I did. But I still knew that I needed to be able to try out an idea and for it possibly to fail. So I got my head down and enjoyed the exercise of digging away quietly until the Saddam Hussein poem was completed. Only once I'd typed it up (and practised reading it) did I ring my friend and perform it for him. So I didn't really risk failing in front of him, because I was pretty sure he'd like it — and he did, and I felt good about myself. But I am learning to be free to fail — honest!

And lastly...
I didn't sit down and analyse what the key factors were!

These elements of starting where we are, playfulness, time, perseverance, freedom to fail and not being too self conscious about it all, were crucial. Take another example, written around the same time (this one has a more obvious Christian content). I started where I was, on the sofa. I had a little time to sit and think, and soon I looked at my watch and spotted that the date was the eighth of August 1992, an idea nudged my elbow and asked, "Can Rob come out to play?" So I did...

All The Eights, Eighty Eight
(August 1992)

This is true:
On the 8th of the 8th 1980
I spent 8 pounds 88 on a watch.
Why didn't I remember that 4 years ago?
On the 8th of the 8th '88?
I would've so enjoyed saying;
"On the 8th of the 8th 1980
I spent 8 pounds 88 on a watch.
It was 8 years ago to the day."
But I can't.
'Cos I missed it.
What was I doing?
Where was I going?
Was I really so busy
I didn't have time to look at my watch
And spot the date?

How many more, more significant moments
Have I bulldozed my way through?
No way of knowing which cobwebs I've crushed
As the JCB of my busyness drones on
And unwittingly drowns

A dodo's best song,
A child's first cry,
A friend's last try,
God's answer to "Why?"
I'll never be there again to hear it,
If on the very day,
The very date,
The very hour,
The very moment that it comes
I don't hear it.
And the JCB of my busyness drones on.

If I'd not made a conscious decision to take some time I probably wouldn't have heard the idea. But now that I was wondering "How many hidden messages does God cram into one day?" My ears were more alert when the next idea happened...

All The Eights, Eighty Eight (part two)
(August 1992)

This is also true:
The computer I wrote this up on
And the printer I printed this out on
If you include VAT and the delivery fee
Came to 888 pounds and 88p
That's poetry, to the penny!
And I heard.
Even I couldn't miss that one!
Sometimes God helps by raising his voice.

Once you've started, ideas often take on a life of their own and you can't help but write them. You make connections that you would never have made otherwise. They may not mean that much to somebody else, but this was a discovery I made, and it was special for me, it was mine.

But for every time you make a connection, there are other times when nothing happens. Times when we're tempted to think we shouldn't have wasted our time and just got on with the jobs that still need to be done. That's the whole problem with creative ideas — you can't control them. You can't get them to turn up on time, you can't tie them down so that you'll know where to find them the next time.

All The Eights, Eighty Eight (part three)
(September 1992)

A month later,
I was flicking through Dillons,
I realised what I was doing
On the 8th of the 8th, '88
Why I was elsewhere
Why I wasn't quite head square.

I was so tearful
So totally touched
By the birth of Beatty
Princess Beatrice
Born to the family of Fergie
On the 8th of the 8th '88
At 8.18 in the morning
Ten minutes late!

But then her mum never was one
For fitting in with the way other people wanted things to read.

Because you can't tie them down, that makes it all the more wonderful when they do turn up completely unexpected. Why would you want to tie down something like this? Because we're scared they might not fly, or because we're scared they might? It's so much more exhilarating to let it fly, and to enjoy watching it swoop and soar. It's a feeling that you know you'd never have had if you hadn't stopped to think about that first idea, and then that second idea came, and, OK, you felt a bit disillusioned after that, but now the whole thing seems to be getting somewhere and you're not sure what's going to happen next, but your senses are more alive than they've been for years.

All The Eights, Eighty Eight (part four)
(September 1992)

The other day
I was driving to Cardiff
And my milometer hit the 88,888 miles.
Eighty eight thousand, eight hundred and eighty eight miles.

I don't know what that means.
Just thought I'd mention it.

Sometimes you can try too hard! Which, of course, gives you vital practice in being free to fail. Whenever you create something new there's a risk. Very rarely does an idea come completely sorted, packaged and presented. Most of the time all you know is that you've touched the top of something. Then you have to decide whether to dig. Is it a chest of gold or an old shopping trolley? You can't know. If you never dig, you'll never get the gold, but if you always dig you have to be prepared to find a load of old trolleys. But your digging technique will probably improve, your muscles will develop, and you may even begin to sense the best places to dig, but you'll still come up with some junk. It's all part of the process.

So it depends how we dig. Work away at it quietly, see it as a game, and learn to enjoy the actual exercise of digging, sensing God's pleasure in our endeavours. Then it matters less what we find. This lightness is so important. Without it, it'll be too painful to fail, and sooner or later we'll stop digging. Or, to revert back to the original metaphor: our soil will become hardened and the seed ideas will have little chance of growing.

But sometimes you've landed on an idea and you've not got time to work on it immediately. It's crucial that we find a way of capturing this idea, otherwise it'll float away. Keeping a notebook of observations, snippets of overheard conversations and beginnings of ideas not only gets you ahead of the game in terms of ideas for the future, but often the act of stopping and writing, slows you down long enough to reflect on what the idea could become. If you haven't even got time to stop and write it down, then use a dictaphone. Then, when you've time, transfer the ideas into your notebook.

Often when I need to come up with a new idea, a previous idea calls out from a notebook: "Use me, I'm perfect for this!" The *Happy Families* story on page 122 is an example of this. The story is half way between a Brand New Idea and one I'd Thought Of Before But Never Written Up. I'd heard the story of the one metre long chopsticks many times, but I'd never thought of making it into a sketch, until I needed an idea on the theme of co-operation. Once I began working it began to evolve, and I incorporated the riddle idea which was an unused idea from a previous notebook.

Once you've uncovered an idea and decided it will serve the purpose at hand, how do you develop it? You've just dug it up fresh from the ground, or dusted it down stale from your notebook, but how do you clean it up and make it presentable? One approach is to ask questions of it. By asking the simple questions *Who? Where? What? When? How?* and *Why?* you will be exercising Craft — a vital component in any creative act. Of course there is no inspiration in Craft itself, the inspiration comes from the way you answer the questions:

Who are the characters?
   Real or fictional? Serious or funny? Caricature or rounded?

Where did it take place?
   Indoors or outdoors, this country or abroad, in a volcano or on a boat?

What is the story?
   What happens?

When did the story happen?
   Last week, one thousand years ago, thirty years into the future?

How is it best told?
   Song, poem, story, sketch? With or without action? A specific genre?

Why tell it?
   To warn, to challenge, to encourage, to entertain? All four and more?

As you go through the rest of the book, you'll see many examples of the results of asking these simple questions of an idea.

There is a limit to the number of old ideas you can adapt. What if you've not been keeping a notebook? What if you have to suddenly come up with new, creative ideas? The five principles mentioned before don't guarantee new ideas, they simply provide the atmosphere in which new ideas are more likely to occur. So how do new ideas happen?

Recently I've been reading a book by Edward de Bono on lateral thinking, which gives some answers (*Serious Creativity*, by HarperCollins Publishers). I was attracted to it by a review in the

Times Educational Supplement, which read: "A very useful book. Dr de Bono does not claim to be able to turn us all into Miltons, da Vincis and Einsteins... but his techniques provide an alternative to just sitting around waiting for the Muse to appear." It's a fascinating book. I've recognised some things I do already, and discovered some completely new things which I'm now beginning to put into practice.

When I use the term lateral thinking you might be thinking of those infuriating puzzles that have us tormented for hours — the ones with a dead man lying in a pool of water in a room with no windows or doors holding a burnt match stick in his hand. (Please don't try to work out the answer to this — I made it up!) These riddles are only one part of lateral thinking, that of problem solving. Another major aspect is the generation of new ideas. As de Bono says: "Lateral thinking is directly concerned with insight and with creativity. But whereas both these processes are usually only recognised after they have happened, lateral thinking is a deliberate way of using information in order to bring them about."

In lateral thinking terms, the *Addicted* monologue (see page 128) works because it is an alternative arrangement of an established set of information. It's a fairly standard sketch formula which I merely adapted to the brief I was staring in the face. Of course, it's not that you can't find new ideas without knowing the techniques and principles. It's more that, knowing this stuff, you're more likely to know where to look to find them. You get a sense of where to start digging for treasure.

But if all this lateral thinking theory sounds like too much hard work, and therefore likely to make you lose the sense of play — then just keep experimenting with new angles, keep asking "What if...?" Keep scribbling ideas and possibilities into your notebook and see what happens. If it doesn't sound like too much work and it's exactly what you think you need, then do you really expect me to just copy out his ideas? That would be both very uncreative and illegal, neither of which is especially appealing.

Introducing the Writes of Passage

The next three chapters provide example script material which you are welcome to use, and reflections on how these ideas happened. At the foot of each script you'll find a principle which can be drawn from this idea, and suggestions as to how you can springboard from this script to producing your own ideas. As a general point, I'm sure that most of the ideas would lend themselves to being told by one person as a story, so just because some are currently in a sketch format doesn't mean that they can't be adapted and retold in a way that suits both your style and your circumstances.

The scripts (or Writes of Passage) along this journey have been divided into three parallel paths in order to make the whole journey easier to follow. In each section you will be able to trace the progression of ideas and styles that was occurring, and how these propelled me toward the views outlined in the conclusion of this book. My hope is that by being honest about the process, you'll understand both that the ideas are based on genuine experience, and that these ideas are offered humbly since I'm fully aware that I've been slow to learn.

The structure is a response to the frequently asked question: "Where do ideas come from?" I hope that by dividing the material according to its source, *ie* where the idea came from, the progression of ideas is clearer, and the stimulus for you creating your own ideas stronger.

The three groups of material are as follows:

1   Material inspired by the Bible
2   Material inspired by my own stories
3   Material inspired by other people's stories.

There will be elements of inreach, upreach and outreach in all three strands of my journey. You will need to weigh up which pieces are suitable to be lifted and used in different contexts. Some pieces are included for use in outreach situations, some are included with the aim of inspiring you to write your own version of the same type of idea, and others are only included to provide an example of where new ideas come from and are not designed to be used publicly at all. You must decide which are which!

Just on a point of accuracy, the writing process before 1989 sometimes involved the other writing member of Trapdoor Theatre Company — Alun John. The material dated after 1989 I have to take full responsibility for! You should also be aware that sketches in particular are very difficult to read. So, you may wish to skim through these and on to the next part of the journey. The priority is that you remain with me on my journey and that this helps you to make progress on yours.

The Bible as Source

The Bible as Source

The Bible is a huge resource of ideas. It's full of characters, ideas, radical statements and, of course, wonderful stories. A significant part of the journey we're about to embark on has been grappling with how best to use parables in outreach. How much should they be explained? To what extent should their meaning be spelled out? How do you steer people toward finding the meaning Jesus would want them to find? You'll see how my thinking on this has developed as the journey progresses.

The starting point was the Bible. Our church youth group was full of wild and wacky characters, and our youth leader chose to channel our considerable energy by getting us into drama. The instinctive approach was to put together new versions of well-known Bible stories. Our rough and (almost) ready productions used loads of humour, energy and were great fun to do and, we were told, to watch.

These skits were never written down. We just busked our way through the story line and shoe-horned in as many gags as we could along the way. We knew little about dramatic structure, less about literature and we thought that art and craft was what kids did with cardboard and glue when the grown-ups had run out of stories! But this ignorance was actually to our advantage. I'm sure if we'd had any idea how little we knew we wouldn't have had the gall to be so liberated. Raw energy, a sense of fun and the feeling that we were "doing drama" meant that the whole thing was wonderfully free and unique to us. We started from where we were, and it seemed to work.

Once we'd realised that we could say something here we had a problem: what was it that we wanted to say? Well, what we should say of course. But this time we took the tea towels off our heads and brought the Bible situations up-to-date.

Good News
(1985)

(Newspaper journalist sitting at his desk on phone to a contact.
Fisherman enters to make the conversation three-way.)

Journalist   Look I'm a journalist, of course I've heard the
rumours. That's why I'm phoning you; I knew you'd
have both ears to the ground, if you see what I
mean... Good, so what've you got?... Yeah... Yeah...
That's what I like to hear... Of course I didn't, I knew
they were just wild rumours, but I like to hear what
the people are saying... Right, so you'll let me know
when you hear where they've hidden the body...
(Laughs) Yeah it's not only how do you lose a corpse,
but it's a case of where to look when you've lost
one... Embarrassing!...

Fisherman   (Barging in) I want to speak to someone on the Jesus
case.

Journalist   (To F) Yes? (To phone) No I'm still here...

Fisherman   Are you doing the Jesus story?

Journalist   (To F) Who wants to know?

Fisherman   I do.

Journalist   Obviously... (To phone)... Hang on a second... (To F)
You'll have to hang on, this phone call's important.
(To phone)... Sorry about that...

Fisherman   (Interrupting) The rumours are true! Jesus is back!

Journalist   (To F) Oh give me a break... (To phone)... What? Not
you. No, I'm not getting shirty with you, there's this
fisherman in the office. Seriously, I can smell him.

Fisherman   Will you listen to me. Jesus is alive and well. He
spoke to me.

Journalist   (To phone) He spoke to him... to Jesus... I'll ask him
(To F) Are you all right?

Fisherman   Yes, I'm all right.

Journalist   (To phone) He's all right... No, he says he's all right.
No, not that Jesus is all right, that he's all right.

Fisherman   That's what I'm saying. Jesus is all right.

Journalist   (To phone) And Jesus is all right. They're both all
right, all right?

Fisherman   About thirty of us have seen him so far.

Journalist	(To phone) There's about thirty of them... No not in the office. About thirty of them have seen him... (To F) And they're all right? (To phone) Don't start that again... (To F) He doesn't believe you.
Fisherman	(Raising his voice) Well if he's not dead, who's got the body then?
Journalist	(To phone) Did you hear that?... (To F) The Romans.
Fisherman	Funny, I don't see them parading it round the streets.
Journalist	(To phone) Try again... (To F) The priests maybe?
Fisherman	Ask him, if the priests had it doesn't he think they'd produce it?
Journalist	(To F) Course they would. (To phone) If the priests had it, don't you think they'd produce the body... (To F) Unless the disciples stole the body.
Fisherman	What about the guards?
Journalist	(To F) What about the guards? Ah...! (To phone) What about the guards?... (To F) No, they wouldn't have it.
Fisherman	No. (Trying to stay patient) How did a bunch of civilians get past the crack temple guards at the tomb?
Journalist	(To F) You're good at this aren't you. (To phone) Ready for this one? How did they steal the body when the temple guards were there?... (To F) They were asleep?
Fisherman	Is he serious?
Journalist	(To phone) Are you serious?... (To F) He's serious.
Fisherman	Well ask him, is the tomb empty?
Journalist	(To phone) Is the tomb empty?... (To F) Yes it's empty.
Fisherman	Ask him, has anyone got the body?
Journalist	(To phone) Has anyone got the body?... (To F) No, no one's got the body.
Fisherman	Well ask him, how can he ignore the evidence?
Journalist	(To phone) How can you ignore the evidence?
Fisherman	Ask him... No, I'll ask him. (Takes phone) What can I do to make you believe me, I've seen him... Hello?... He hung up!

Principle:	Take a Bible event and modernise it (ie ask when and where it is set).
Springboard:	What other Bible events would lend themselves to modernisation?

As you can see this sketch is basically dramatised apologetics and it worked well enough, especially with an audience who still needed some persuading about the use of drama to draw out Bible principles. We kept it simple, direct and rooted in the Bible, like the following sketch, inspired by the passage where it talks about the angels not fully understanding what it means to be redeemed.

Scramble Scramble

(1989)

(Two First World War flying ace types, with particularly stiff upper lips. The account of Normal Harry can be performed with live guitar and large cartoon picture cards. It should be performed with good pace and appropriate voices for the different characters. It could feasibly be performed by a cast of more than two people.)

Winko	Scramble, scramble. Angel 7984 to stand by, await further orders.
Binki	Roger Winko. Bandit at 12 o'clock, he's proceeding into her flat... Confirming, the last bus has gone... Yes sir, it's Gold Blend coffee! Bandit switching off main light, looks as if I'm going to have to go in and bail her out, awaiting instructions, please advise.
Winko	Control will advise, scramble, scramble. Angel 3743 to stand by with ground support. Prepare to have mother phone the flat.
Binki	Update: Bandit choosing Lionel Ritchie album.
Winko	Angel 3743 is standing by the phone.
Binki	Danger imminent, bandit's hand on knee.
Winko	3743, I don't care if mother is in the bath! Get her to the phone!
Binki	We're going to have to move in.
Winko	Give her time. She has a mind of her own.
Binki	Situation critical.
Winko	A few more seconds, let her decide.
Binki	It's alright. She's slapped his hand. Bandit retreating.
Winko	Angel 3743 stand down. Well done 7984.
Binki	Thank you sir, but is was her decision.
Winko	Stand down 7984.
Binki	Standing down sir. (Move to a more relaxed, off-duty atmosphere)

Winko	Well Binki, how's eternal life treating you?
Binki	Source of endless satisfaction thank you sir.
Winko	And how's Mrs Binki?
Binki	She's on cloud nine sir.
Winko	Please, do drop the "sir", Binki.
Binki	Well, I just thought, with the recent promotion sir, uh, Winko.
Winko	More of a sideways move, different skills, different assignments. Mind you I quite miss all this front line stuff.
Binki	What have you been assigned to Winko?
Winko	Stock taking essentially. Compiling an inventory of, oh shall we call them "blessings of a spiritual nature."
Binki	What does that involve then?
Winko	Scouring the heavenlies for every possible spiritual advantage, listing them in alphabetical order and establishing a comprehensive network of cross references.
Binki	So it's a list then?
Winko	Quite a list too.
Binki	I doubt if the humans deserve half of it.
Winko	Quite, and that's exactly what we're going to tell Him, isn't it.
Binki	(To audience) By heavens, I think he's serious. (Both enter the Lord's presence, looking nervous)
Winko	Lord. May I draw your attention to Normal Harry, (picture card 1) presently under the jurisdiction of Angel 5864. He grew up in a nice enough home.
Harry	Hello Mum
Mum	Hello Harry
Harry	Hello Dad
Dad	Hello son.
Winko	(Picture 2, inane grin) Life was fine, until at the age of 7, he deliberately stole Edward Higginbottom's gob stopper. (Picture 3, with Edward)
Edward	Give me that, sucker.
Harry	No. (Slap) Oww!
Winko	These were the first steps down the road of his averagely sinful life. By the age of 14 he was smoking. (Picture card showing all three vices)

Harry	(Cough)
Winko	Drinking.
Harry	Gis a drink.
Winko	And going to loud parties.
Harry	My brain hurts.
Winko	But then he got thrown out of the Boys Brigade, and took up knitting for a while. But against his parents' advice, his vice continued. (Picture 5, parents nagging)
Mum	Don't do that son.
Harry	(Cough)
Dad	If I've told ya once...
Harry	You have.
Mum	Turn that music down.
Harry	What?
Winko	(Picture 6, with bikers) At the age of 18 he was running with the wrong crowd and ended up in Peckham with a stitch.
Harry	Who are you looking at?
Biker	Stitch that!
Harry	Ooowww!!
Winko	This is where you stepped in. And saved him from his miserable self. (Picture 7, Harry with a halo)
Harry	I am H-A-P-P-Y.
Winko	Once he had, as they say, given his heart to you.
Harry	(Heartbeat sound effect)
Winko	He tried to rejoin the Boys Brigade but he couldn't fit into the trousers and everyone laughed at him. Strangely he blamed you for this persecution. (Picture 8, Harry shaking his fist toward heaven)
Harry	Why me God?
Winko	And this new found vice of passing the buck upwards took a grip. Although you had given everything for him, he would say:
Harry	God doesn't love me.
Winko	Although you had made him your son and heir, he would say:
Harry	I'm worthless.
Winko	Although you'd provided all he could ever need, he still thought living for you was too tough.
Harry	It's too tough.

Winko	And at the age of 36, he's as pitiful as ever.
Harry	Oh, woe is me.
Winko	And it's on these grounds that I come to you with the following suggestions. Having compiled a comprehensive list of spiritual blessings I would say the problem is that they are spoilt. They've been given too much, and they don't appreciate you as they should. So I've taken the liberty to make some changes to the spiritual blessings on said list. For example, I suggest enrolling them as slaves, not sons, thereby ensuring loyalty and obedience. Or to promise to be with them, but not commit yourself to being sealed inside them — thus providing a loophole for you to pull out in the event of gross and deliberate sin. We feel these, and the other changes will ensure a more responsible attitude from your people. (Listens to God's response through headphones) Yes, thank you sir, very happy sir... Good, thank you sir... Well it did take me quite some time to compile it all... A pleasure sir... Fine... May I ask why sir?... That's good enough for me sir.
Binki	What did he think of the suggestions?
Winko	He found them "interesting."
Binki	And?
Winko	He still wants to give them everything.
Binki	What?
Winko	He said "How could a father not want the best for his children?" He wants them to have everything.
Binki	That's good enough for me.
Winko	Quite. (Both salute and freeze)

❏	**Principle:**	Take a Bible phrase ("angels don't understand") and ask What if...?
❏	**Springboard:**	What other style (if not World War I pilots) could this idea be written in? (ie ask Who are the characters, and Where is it set?)

Quite direct really, wasn't it? There had always been something about the parables that intrigued me, such as Jesus' story in Luke 14, which tells of different peoples' excuses for not coming to The Feast. What would be the modern equivalents of "I cannot come to the feast for I

have just married a cow"? This time the all important explanation bit
was worked in gradually as the story unfolded.

Juggling Jack
(1989)

There once was a man called Juggling Jack
Who juggled well, he'd got the knack.
He threw those clubs up in the air
And when they fell his hands were there.

People came from miles around
Whenever Jack was in their town.
He'd show them tricks right through the day
Then he'd turn to the crowd and, he'd say:
Go ahead
Who us?
Yes have a go, I'll teach you all you need to know
I'll even let you come along
And teach you how to sing this song:

(Sing) Get down, turn around, stand up and follow me.
Get down, turn around, stand up and follow me.
That's the bit you join in with!

(audience participation prep)

Now the crowd just smiled and turned away
And said to each other: "Uh uh, no way."
Excuses flowed from every tongue
From the tall to the short, from the old to the young.

The story's not new, 'cos years ago
A man said "Come" but the crowd said "No"
People thought he was insane,
Just goes to show — things don't change.

Back with Jack who was trying to tell
This man that juggling was really swell
He'd caught a guy, who was rushing by
Grabbed his arm, looked him straight in the eye.

Go ahead
(Welsh accent) Who me?
Yes have a go, I'll teach you all you need to know
But I've tried it once and it didn't work
When the clubs hit your head it really hurts
But there'd be no pain if you had caught.
It's obvious, you've not been taught
If you give me a chance I'll prove you wrong
And show you how to sing this song:

(sing) Get down, turn around, stand up and follow me.
(and repeat)

Now remember that man from years ago
Who the people thought was "weirdo"
He raised the dead and fed the poor
But they, did say, that they had tried before.

Meanwhile back at Jugglesville
Good old Jack was going in for the kill:

Go ahead
(Lancashire accent) Who me?
Yes, have a go, I'll show you all you need to know
Don't waste my time, I'm a busy guy
Gotta go, gotta do, gotta see, gotta buy.
But sir, said Jack, there ain't no cost
It'll cost me time son, get lost.
Learning clubs will take too long
I've got no time to sing your song:

(sing) Get down, turn around, stand up and follow me.
(and repeat)

Now Jesus said he'd give them peace
From busy lives they'd find release
But the people thought that they were fine
And they, did say, they did not have the time.

Now our man Jack the juggling king
Was gossiping about the juggling thing

He'd talk away, through the day
And this is what Jack did say:

Go ahead
(Belfast accent) Who me?
Yes, have a go, I'll teach you all you need to know
Just go away, he said with a sneer
I have no need of your juggling gear.
But sir, said Jack, there ain't no cost
I'll say it once son, get lost.
And as he turned and walked away
Juggling Jack could hear him say
Life's just fine, there's nothing wrong
I've got no need to sing your song:

(sing) Get down, turn around, stand up and follow me.
(and repeat)

Now Jesus said he'd love them still
If they followed him, or if they shouted "Kill"
But as his blood began to flow
They did say they did not want to know.

Now Jack was sad that much was clear
'Cos the people didn't want to hear
He'd nearly packed his clubs away
When a friend came along... when a good friend came along
...When a good friend who Jack worked with came along and Jack
heard him say:

(Devon accent)
I've been watching you with your juggling and that,
and well you've never pushed it on me or nothing but I was
thinking I'd like to try, well I'd like to talk about it
anyway, see there's loads of questions, like, does it hurt
your fingers? Do you ever drop them and make a fool of
yourself? And do you ever feel like giving up altogether...

And they talked, long and hard into the night, and because Jack knew
him well he listened and answered honestly and in good time his mate
decided "I think I'll give it a go."

❏	**Principle:**	Take one of Jesus' parables and change the metaphor (ie ask What?), change the setting (ie ask Where?) and the time (ie ask When?)
❏	**Springboard:**	What other metaphor (not juggling) could be used and what excuses would people give then?

Again, pretty clear, certainly by the end. I'm still not sure whether this tendency to spell it out was a result of our own insecurity or whether it was simply what the audience required. On the one hand, I was insecure enough to need to be seen to have something to say, but then the audience also needed reassuring that something was being said. At this time there seemed little value to a poem that was just a bit of fun, not in a church service anyway. Or even a poem that had a deeper meaning but deliberately left the meaning a little obscure. This would require the audience to be willing to work it out for themselves, which they might not be willing or able or expecting to do. We worked on the principle that if they don't have ears to hear, no problem — we'll shout!

Of course, being brought up in the Brethren, I knew that Jesus regularly left his parables unexplained. I knew that he had the confidence to know that those who had ears to hear, would hear. I knew that for those who understood, it would mean so much more because they'd found it for themselves. I knew that Jesus was wonderfully free from what other people thought of him. But I also knew that Jesus didn't need his listeners to book him again for his next show! So I spelt it out... slowly... in capital letters. But in this next piece, I delayed the explanation until the end, therefore hopefully drawing the listeners into wanting to know who this character is.

I Was Fine
(June 1992)

I could cope with it; my "condition."
I'd come to terms with what I was:
The stench, the pus, the filth,
I was getting through the days.
I wasn't happy.
But then who's happy?
I was just as effective with two fingers missing;

I could still show them how I felt!
I could damage myself to my heart's discontent
And do you think it made a difference?
Do donkeys dance?
Maybe they do.
I don't know.
I could dole out the damage
And the scars would soon merge
Could cut myself,
Burn myself,
And earn myself the right to be ugly inside too.

The only thing I knew how to feel
Was sorry for myself.

Then he went and healed me
Me and nine others.

Now I'm no longer numb.
No, now I feel pain.
Now I know pain.
Why did he heal me?
Why didn't he leave me?

I didn't ask to be beautiful?
I didn't ask to be whole?

He said "Now feel joy, really feel joy."
But all I feel is pain.
He said, he knew about pain.

But it's easier, numb.
Before the pain
I was getting through the days.
I wasn't happy.
But then who's happy?

And you ask me why I didn't go back to thank him?

> | | **Principle:** | Take an event from the gospels and imagine yourself as one of the characters who meet Jesus. |
> | --- | --- | --- |
> | | **Springboard:** | What gospel event has always attracted you? Which character would you be? What would you say to Jesus? What would he say to you? |

A long time after writing this I discovered that, without knowing it, I'd used an approach borrowed from Ignatius Loyola. I'd used my imagination to project myself back into an event in the gospels and drawn some practical fruit from it. This was particularly helpful to me, since I'd been brought up with these stories and they'd become a little too familiar. This approach had provided me with a new angle and a personal application and so it had become fresh again. This in turn allowed me to admit my tendency toward preferring numbness, but also to recognise my longing (on many levels) to touch and be touched.

The next piece was inspired by the structure of one of the Psalms. I'd been working my way through the Psalms and had arrived at number 111 which, I read in the footnotes, was an acrostic poem. This means that each line of the Psalm begins with a successive letters of the Hebrew alphabet. It got me thinking — what would a summary of my life sound like using this structure? (This piece would also fit into the section of our own stories as source material. I include this piece here as an example of a structure that might help you in your inreach and upreach. It's also probably a little heavy for some contexts, so do use your wisdom.)

Why?
(December 1992)

(Live = live character, Pos = Positive thoughts, Neg = Negative thoughts. Possibly done to a recorded backing track of the Pos and Neg characters, ideally coming from opposite speakers.)

Pos & Neg	Able, active, aims, ambitions, adrenaline... attacked
Pos & Neg	Busyness; building, bustling, briefing
Live	Be better, no buts, be better, better be better
Pos	Battling
Neg	Bleeding
Pos	But bluffing
Neg	Blind man's bluff

Live	Believe it, be better
Pos	Break up
Neg	The black hole beckons
Pos	Breakdown
Neg	And black holes suck
Live	But, but...
Live	...Can't crumble — career!
Neg	Couldn't care, callous
Live	Cut costs, can do it
Pos	Couldn't cope, careless
Live	Cut corners, can't cancel
Neg	'Cos cancer not caught corrodes
Live	Can't cry, can't cry
Live	Don't. Don't cry, don't die, defy it and do it. Drive through it.
Pos	Danger, don't drive
Live	Drive through it
Pos	Darkness
Live	Drive through it
Pos	Disaster
Neg	Disaster
Pos	Dying
Live	Don't die
Neg	Dying
Live	Don't die
Pos	Dead
Neg	Dead
Live	Dead
Neg	Deserved it
Live	Didn't
Neg	Deserved it
Live	Didn't
Neg	Empty
Live	Lost everything
Pos	Not everything
Neg	Empty room
Pos	Not everything
Neg	Empty chair

Pos	Even now
Neg	Empty life
Pos	Not ended
Neg	On the edge
Pos	Even when
Neg	Everything gone
Pos	Eventually
Live	Feel faint, feel faded
	(Spoken over the next 8 lines) Falling, fear, find faith, find faith, blind faith, blind faith in the fog
Neg	Futile, failure
Pos	He felt it
Neg	Felt futile?
Pos	He felt it
Neg	Felt failure? He never felt failure. Did he drive through the fog?
	Forget it. He never felt failure. Blind...
Pos	...Faith in the fog
Live	Blind faith in the fog
Pos	Follow the lights in front
Live	Grit
Live	Hide me, help me, hold me, hug me (Repeated over next 7 lines)
Pos	Still hope, you'll cope
Neg	Still hope? Hype!
Pos	He's been here
Neg	How?
Pos	He has
Neg	Say how!
Pos	He hears
Live	Hear me, and hold me
Neg	"I", that's all you've got
Pos	No more "I", just Him
Live	Just me
Neg	Just sulk
Live	Just me

Pos	Just think
Neg	Just die
Live	Must I?
Pos	Jeremiah says: "In days to come you'll understand this."
Neg	Jeremiah?
Pos	"In days to come you'll understand this."
Live	Just suppose...
Pos	Knock and the door will be opened
Neg	Kick it down
Pos	No key, just knock
Neg	Kick it through
Pos	Learning a lesson
Neg	Learning?
Pos	Learning a lot
Neg	Liar
Live	Lonely
Neg	Listen
Pos	Living with memories
Live	Memories
Neg	Live with mistakes
Pos	No
Neg	Meaning?
Pos	Now. Living with now
Live	Living with now
Neg	OK, but...
Neg	...People will point
Live	Please!
Neg	Prying, poking, people will push
Live	Leave me in peace
Neg	Perhaps "pieces"?
Pos	Prophesy puts it: "In days to come you'll understand this."
Live	Pain
Neg	Pouring in

Live	Pain
Neg	Beyond swearing
Live	Pain
Pos	Perfects
Neg	Patronising. Questions
Live	When?
Pos	Quiet
Neg	Questions
Live	How?
Pos	Quiet
Neg	Questions
Live	Why?
Pos	Quiet. Quiet...
Pos	...Repent...
Live	So much, so sorry, such shame, so sorry
Neg	And slip, from shame to self pity
Live	So sorry, so stupid, so stupid
Neg	Show them how sorry, show them, scare them
Live	I'm scared
Neg	You're scarred, so show them — suici...
Pos	(Interrupting) Shut up.
Live	I'm slipping
Pos	Stay stable
Live	I'm sickening
Pos	Stay sane
Live	Stay with me
Pos	Take shape
Live	To teach me
Pos	Take time
Live	To turn me
Neg	To tension. To turn your attention to tearing
Pos	Or turn that tearing...
Pos	...to undo the undaring, to move the uncaring to uphold the unsteady, to understand
Live	To understand
Pos & Live	"In days to come you will understand."
Live	How to do the unexpected. To free the unfree, to be uniquely me...

Live	...Not to have to do "V"...
Live	...Why not? Why not "U" straight to double "U"
Neg	And then on to "Y"
Live	I want to know why
Pos	Wait and you'll be waited on
Live	Ask and it... knock and the door... seek and you'll...
Pos & Live	Wait and you'll be waited on
Neg	Words all words
Pos	Wait. Without words. — But why?
Pos	To excel not exist
Live	But why, when...
Pos	To excite and exceed
Neg	To exhaust. And so to "Why"
Pos	"Yes" starts with a "Y"
Live	And I'm asking "Why, when I die have I lived?"
Pos	To say "Yes"
Live	"Yes" starts with a "Y" And yes, I say "Yes" to you
Live	Yes, yesterday still hurts Yes, today still needs stillness But there's something after why, I just don't know what... yet But, "In days to come..."

❏ **Principle:**	Take an established structure and work within this.
❏ **Springboard:**	How would your life read as an acrostic poem? How would your last year read? What other structures might be used?

This piece gave me a chance to say Yes to God. To acknowledge that I didn't know the future, but to say Yes anyway, because I chose to believe that God was in control. It was one of those big moments along the journey — definitely a Write of Passage.

The Ten Commandments

(March 1993)

(First version to be read or recited in a stern, threatening attitude, implying that if you disobey, there'll be serious consequences.)

Voice 1   You won't have any other gods before me
                     You won't have any idols
                     You won't misuse the name of your God
                     You will keep the Lord's day holy
                     You will honour your parents
                     You won't murder
                     You won't commit adultery
                     You won't steal
                     You won't lie
                     You won't covet your neighbour's possessions
                     You won't.
                     You just won't.

(Second version to be read or recited in gentle, positive attitude, implying that the character fully expects you to keep the commandments, and is enthusiastic about your likelihood of succeeding in this.)

Voice 2   You won't have any other gods before me
                     You won't have any idols
                     You won't misuse the name of your God
                     You will keep the Lord's day holy
                     You will honour your parents
                     You won't murder
                     You won't commit adultery
                     You won't steal
                     You won't lie
                     You won't covet your neighbour's possessions
                     You won't.
                     You just won't.

Narrator   In which voice have you always heard them?

❑	**Principle:**	You don't have to be clever with words to be able to write.
❑	**Springboard:**	What other ways could you hear the Ten Commandments? What other statements could be heard in different ways?

For a different version of the same idea turn to *Counting Backwards From Ten* on page 93. This poem was the product of something I was wrestling with at the time... as you'll see.

Another passage that attracted my attention at the time was the one where James talks about faith and actions in chapter two of his letter. This is what came.

The Perfect Sketch
(April 1993)

(As this introduction takes place the rest of the cast bring on the set and props for the sketch. At first these should be quite orthodox, but they can become increasingly bizarre building to highly comical by the end.)

Introducer   Ladies and gentlemen, by way of introduction to the next sketch, I'd like to say that this is probably the most complete sketch I've ever seen. It has everything; pace, energy, pathos, comedy and a depth of meaning I'm still only in the process of fully appreciating. Some sketches tend too much on word-play, and leave the audience punch drunk with words. Other sketches rely too much on visual symbolism and swamp the audience with a wash of images that may well make sense to the performers, but rarely trigger anything but confusion or frustration in the watchers.

But this sketch manages somehow to combine the verbal and the visual to engage the audience on all levels. We believe that each one of you here this evening, whether primarily a thinker or a feeler will find themselves completely captivated, both tonight and for years to come. It deals with its subject in such a simple yet profound way. All too often such subjects are dealt with clumsily and only serve to further the guilt we all sense when looking at this theme. Too many times have I seen material which only leaves me even more apathetic, but this sketch seems only able to inspire people to practical action. Quite a feat.

Without giving anything away, it highlights how we tend to get bogged down in talking about such issues, and somehow manage to avoid actually doing anything.

Cast:	(Ready in position) So are we going to do the sketch then?
Introducer	What? No. I've just told them all about it. We don't need to do it. (Exits. Cast collect and remove all props and leave stage embarrassed.)

❑ **Principle:**	Illustrate a biblical principle by taking it to an opposite extreme. Visual ideas stay in the memory.
❑ **Springboard:**	What other warnings in the Bible could be similarly portrayed?

Again a very clear explanatory conclusion. The next piece happened when I was asked by a friend in Springs Dance Company to help them out at a performance. They'd put together a series of dance pieces on The Parable of the Sower, and they needed someone to read the appropriate passages before each dance to set the scene.

The trouble was that no matter how slowly I read the passage, it just didn't take long enough to allow them to change. So they suggested I write a new version of the parable. I tried, but the original is so beautifully succinct that to make it longer just sounded like waffle to keep the audience occupied while the cast changed backstage. Then I thought, maybe I could put it into a free flow poetry style. So I went off and found a quiet corner in a pub down the road and experimented. The outcome seemed to take the right length of time, and I rather liked it!

The Sower
(August 1993)

1   A farmer got up to go to sow
And began to throw the seed across the field
But some seed fell on the footpath

Where feet would crush
And birds rush to eat each last shred.

Later, the teacher said;
The seeds that spread and fed the birds instead
Are the ones who only hear the words in their head
And the evil one comes, and numbs their heart
And keeps them dead.

2   But other seed fell
And when what's sown, lands on stone.
Yes, it might have grown for a while
But the farmer's smile has gone.
For no seed can grow with no soil below.
For no seed is freed from the need for food.

And the teacher said;
His words may bed in the hearts of some for a while
They begin to believe, they receive with joy
'Til the day when troubles come
And trials wile their ruthless way
To their rootless prey
And their faith wanes away.

3   But who is it that warns
The seed that was thrown among thorns?
They grow up together, side by side,
And thorns hide their beguiling smile
And bide their time, until the day
When the field feels a little too small
For them all.
But it's not the thorns that fall.

And the teacher said;
These seeds are the ones who hear
And get so near.
But fear and find
Their mind will wind around
And worries hound, 'til they're gagged and bound
And poked and choked, by worries, wealth
And whether they'll be found wanting.

4   But other seed fell well
    And time was to tell how high the crop would swell
    To thirty fold, or sixty fold, or a hundred fold.

    And the teacher told
    That souls would grow when the seed found the ground
    Where no thorns would bind; no rock, block;
    Or birds flock to pick or peck.
    And he knew
    That good soil would oil the oath,
    Would grace the growth,
    Of the ones who heard the word and understood.

5   Those that have ears to hear, let them hear.
    Those that have eyes to see, let them see.
    Those that have a heart to heal, let them feel.
    But those that will not see, let them be.

❏	**Principle:**	Rephrasing one of Jesus' stories in your own words allows people to hear the familiar in a new way and may give them longer to reflect on its content.
❏	**Springboard:**	How would you retell this parable? Which other parables would you retell in your own voice?

A while later I put some mime/storytelling moves to it and turned it into a performance poem of my own. Now it rounds off my *People Like Me* show. But somehow it still seems strange that such a poignant moment at the end of a show only exists because the girls couldn't get their tights on quickly enough!

I'm sure you noticed that I've retained Jesus' explanation of the parable, which he actually gave later to the disciples, and then only when they pressed him for its meaning. But I was slowly moving toward really believing that those who had ears to hear would hear the meaning of a parable. The next piece was a stepping stone on this particular journey. I thought I was writing a monologue about patience and waiting for God's perfect timing, but as often happens, once you start on an idea it takes on a life of its own. As I wrote, the idea grew into something completely different and, without intending to, I'd written a piece about a subject I wouldn't have dared to deal with.

The Flowers Told On Me

(March 1994)

A week ago I was given some flowers to look after. I have always loved flowers.

On the evening of the first day I watched them. I studied them. Spoke with them. Got to know them. Many were still very young, still in bud. Yet I wanted them to grow. I watched them, but they would not grow.

On the morning and the evening of the second day still I watched them, and still they would not grow. I saw that it was not good. Still they hid from me, still they closed themselves to me. Yes, I wanted them to grow.

On the evening of the third day I watched them and still they kept their promise from me. Yet I wanted them to grow. So I took one. We went to my room and I looked more closely and I saw that this one wanted to grow, wanted to flower. I whispered to her that I would help her grow, for I wanted to see her full grown. So I pulled a petal back and down, carefully. Then another, and another, but she only wept silently, and as I continued to pull her petals off I found no flower inside her bud. I saw that it was not good. For I had not made her grow, but I had destroyed her. And the petals would never return.

On the morning of the fourth day the other flowers saw what I had done to the one I had taken. How I had destroyed her. And they told on me! I had begged them not to, yet still they told on me.

On the morning of the fifth day the ones with the loud voices collected me in the police car. I wanted to bring them with me, for I had been asked to look after them. But they would not let me.

On the morning and the evening of the sixth day the ones with the loud voices shouted at me. They do not like me, so I will not tell them why.

Tomorrow will be the seventh day. I think I will rest then. I am tired and the cuts on my hands hurt (Looks at hands) Look, I still have blood on my hands.

| ❏ | **Principle:** | Once you've started, an idea will often take off. |
| ❏ | **Springboard:** | Just start something, anything. See where it takes you. |

The performing of this sketch was a milestone for me. Because of the way the idea had transformed itself into something else, I wanted to give space for the audience to have the same moment of realisation that I'd had — that wonderful Aha! moment. It was the first time I've ever performed something which wasn't clearly spelt out. Afterwards people came up to me, and seemed to be fascinated by what I was getting at. I did tell them, but only after I'd heard what they thought it was about. I heard quite a range of interpretations, many of which were far more profound than mine! This was certainly new territory.

It was around this time that God first put the question into my head: "Which do you want more — people to think, or people to know what you think?" Tough question. Other tough questions were: "What about all those who didn't come up and ask me what it was about? What about all those who switched off, or thought they were too stupid to get it, or had just had such a hard day that they couldn't be bothered to think?

Well, they're probably the ones who didn't have ears to hear and wouldn't be interested in taking it in even if you gave them direct dictation. Part of the challenge would be to have made it interesting enough for them to want to think it through, or visual enough for it to remain in their memories until a time when they do feel like thinking it through. But ultimately there will still be those that won't or can't hear.

I was thrilled that God had used a parable of mine to speak very clearly to people about issues that were current for them and that I knew nothing about. This was fascinating, and got me mulling over lots of new possibilities in my mind. I was very conscious of my need to be led.

Psalm Twenty Three And A Half

(August 1994)

He's my shepherd
What more could I want?
He makes me lie down in green pastures
He glides me through the still waters
He restores my sullen stolen soul
And pleads with me through the paths of righteousness
For his own namesake's sake.

For his own stake in what he'll make from my life
And how he'll take my walk through the valley of the shadow of death,
Where I will fear no evil breath.
For he is with me
And he brings new birth from the mirth of my enemies
And his rod and his staff lead me home
To his comfort zone
Where he repairs a table before me
– the broken one from the temple –
He makes presents of my enemies
As he anoints my head with oil
And keep that cup steady,
It looks a touch on the full side already!
Surely, goodness and mercy shall follow me close behind
Shall scout for me up ahead
Shall stalk for me as I'm led by my shepherd
All the days, as he raises my life from the horde
And I swell with pride
As I dwell inside
The house of the Lord
For ever.

⊒	**Principle:**	Again, if it has become over familiar, put it in your own words.
⊒	**Springboard:**	Would you re-phrase this Psalm? If so, how? What other passages have lost their freshness for you?

This piece is a similar style to that of *The Sower* — a well known passage of the Bible that I've personalised. Somehow this hybrid of Scripture and self-expression provided a combination of what God was saying to me, and what I wanted to say to him (and myself). It had become a little stale, but this approach allowed me to make it "mine" again. It's not dissimilar to the way in which a jazz musician takes a tune and improvises around it. You never quite lose the feel of the first, but the new interpretation can feel quite different. This will not be to some people's taste, but then neither is jazz: as my mother always says: "Why don't they just play the tune properly?"

As you've seen, this issue of how best to use parables in communication has gripped me over the last five years. Two years ago I decided to put together a show which would apply these principles. This show became "The Prodigal Grandson" which is a retelling of

Jesus' parable in Luke 15. I start the show with a summary of the story as we know it, albeit a little modernised.

The Prodigal Son
(January 1997)

There once was a man who had a father and a brother
And another man who had a father and a brother
And another man who had two sons.
The older son was one for getting things done
And has been called methodical
And the second son was one for having fun
And has been called... The Prodigal.
Now to tell the tale in the time it was told
Takes tea towels, ties, and those togas that leave your
legs go cold.
And anyway you wouldn't want to see my scrawny old legs
So it seems to me that it sits up and begs
To be modernised,
Since it may have become familiarised for some.
So, here we go:

The father had a firm.
In fact he had a factory
And yes, you've guessed or been able to deduce
The product was balloons.
Soon came the terrible day when the second son said to his dad
"Hey dad I've had it up to here with being here
I've got to get away.
I've packed my gear, and sold my stuff
But there's not enough, and I'm sure you know
What dosh I'm due when you finally go... so...
I'd like it now... please."
Well what could the father say?
Well he could say, "Bog off, on your bike, take a ride, take a hike" he
could say.
And he could say, "Yeah, sure, fine, whatever you like" he could say.
But he couldn't say, "Look son, I love you, so of course you must be free
to find
yourself, so even though it'll break my heart, go if you must. But this'll
always be your home."

He couldn't... because... it wouldn't have rhymed.
So he waved his son away and went (make screeching noise with balloon)
Sorry, but it was a very bad day.

The son soon saw that life was the biz with a bag full of cash.
Life was a breeze, life was a bash
It was party time, time and again,
And he gained a reputation for a darn good do.
"Hello, have a drink."
"Hello, have a drink."
"Hello!! have a drink."
"Not now, have a drink."

Some you win and some you have to buy
But you couldn't have met a more generous guy
He loved it
And so did his friends
But there'll always be a crowd
When money talks loud
But the day when the dosh... lost its voice

When all it was was a whisper — people went away,
Friends couldn't stay.
The party was over
And the part he played as rich kid stopped.
He had a job to get a job
So he learned how to hide from the rent man
So he learned how to squat,
Where to beg
What to say

How to stay alive.
"Please, please, please, please.
I've never been this low,
picking through the bins where the people throw their stuff

I can't do this, I've had enough.
I'll hitch-hike home, swallow my pride,
Eating humble pie's more dignified than this."
But his father saw him coming

And came out running
And held him, and held him.
He was home, at last.
He forgave him
And gave him a party to surpass all parties in the past.

But what about his brother, working away for the family firm.
And this was fine until... he stopped
And heard a party begin, without him,
"No dad, I'm not going in, how can you be so rash
As to waste our hard earned petty cash on him.
I don't mean to put him down, but you don't know where he's been".
"True, I don't where he's been, but I do know.
He's been dead, and now he's not
He's been lost and now he's found
He's been away and now he's around again.
And to me, those are grounds... for a party."

Principle:	Change the time setting of a well known story (ie ask When?). Decide what job they do (ie ask Who are they?).	
Springboard:	How would you modernise this parable? What job would you give them? Which other parables lend themselves to being modernised?	

At this point in the show I ask the audience to imagine what would happen next: What if the elder brother had a son? What would his life be like? How would he react if he met his uncle (the original prodigal)? Are his uncle and his dad still speaking to each other? All these questions propel us off on a new story which looks at the same issues as the original — family pressures, the search for fullness of life and the Father love of God — but from a brand new angle.

A while later I was asked to put together some monologues based on the characters from this story. These would provide a focus for a prayer day on the theme of "Bringing back the Prodigals". I adapted some of the lines from the show and produced the following.

Monologues From The Prodigal
(March 1998)

Father

When Jesus first invented us in Luke chapter fifteen, it was incredible to see the effect we were having on our audience. We were being told by the master storyteller — quite a start for any fictional character. Then, of course, I realised that people saw my character as representing God. Quite a challenge! But all the time my youngest was away, I got a glimpse of how God might feel, well a glimpse of a suggestion of how God might feel — it broke my heart. Oh he wrote or phoned every now and then — usually when he needed help, but I missed him, I really missed him.

I almost got to the point of wishing I'd not given him such freedom of choice. All I wanted to do was step in there and sort it all out, but you can't not until he asked anyway. Before that unforgettable hug, I knew that even if he never asked for help, even if he never came back, he'd still be my son... and this would always be his home.

Now that he is back, — it's wonderful. Now I dare to picture my two sons hugging, being brothers again. It hurts, it hurts.

Prodigal

So much for finding "life in all its fullness"! I was physically and mentally exhausted. Then it struck me, I could go back. I'd have money. But I'd also have big brother with all his tutting and frowning — and I still want a full life, despite all this mess, there must be more, but surely not back there with the old party pooper himself. He couldn't enjoy life if it came up and snogged him on the lips.

Though dad would be fine, he's not changed. Every time I "reverse the charges" he says he misses me, and he does, I can hear it. It just doesn't feel like home any more. Besides why should I have to swallow my pride? Huh! Pride in what? In this mess? I don't know why is it so difficult to just stick out my thumb and hitch hike home? "Home" — did I say "Home"?

Brother	I knew it would happen. The waster would come crawling back and father would over-react! But I didn't expect this. First of all he completely writes off his debt — half the family assets mind you, and just as I'd brought the whole thing back to a decent trading profit. And then! Then father insists that we work together. Hasn't he proved beyond doubt that he has no idea about money management? It's as much as I can do to keep tabs on his wild expense account — completely indulgent and wasteful in the extreme! Yes, of course, display the balloons — that's good business practice. But do we really have to have all these parties?

☐	**Principle:**	Filling out the characters from what we know can bring them to life (ie ask "What else would they say?").
☐	**Springboard:**	What would characters from other parables say? What would happen if some of these characters met each other?

It was wonderful to sense God bringing these characters alive in people's minds as people prayed for the 'prodigals' they knew.

Conclusion

So, how can we best use parables in outreach? How much should we spell things out? How much should we leave for people to make their own connections?

The whole process of writing and touring *The Prodigal Grandson* show has been a fascinating experience in wrestling with these questions. My sense, so far, has been to try to find a balance between the two: Not to be so vague as to give people no idea what you're getting at (which usually creates feelings of discomfort), nor for it to be so over-explained as to be patronising or possibly even insulting (which also produces discomfort).

As I've said, in outreach events in the past I would have spelt things out (in capital letters and bold print) leaving the audience very little to think about for themselves. They would have walked out knowing very clearly what I thought, but not necessarily having been challenged as to what they thought — except for a gut feeling as to whether or not they agreed with me. Those who did agree with me (usually the Christians) patted me on the back, pleased that I'd "really let them have it". But those who didn't agree with me, or those who weren't so sure, may well have resented being told what to think. This factor will become increasingly relevant as Post-modernism becomes even more established in our society.

Most audiences are made up of people at so many different stages of faith (or lack of faith) that normal didactic communication is bound to alienate some by saying too much and frustrate others by saying too little. With *The Prodigal Grandson* I've tried to find a balance, to let the story just be a human story, but also to clearly signpost the spiritual dimension as an option that people can choose to consider if they want to. The use of image, symbol, story, and parable allows different people to digest the amount of truth they are ready to take in.

The response, as I've tried out these ideas on the road, has been very interesting. Church people generally tune into the spiritual dynamic, which comes through loud and clear for them. They often come away with a new perspective on God-the-Father's love or other spiritual themes within the story. But it has to be said, they sometimes miss the simple human relationship issues.

The response from unchurched people has varied widely. Many also delve into the spiritual themes in the story, but others steer clear of this area, preferring to focus on the human aspects of the story. Whichever they choose, they appreciate being given this freedom to view the show as they want to, and not as they're told to. They take on the amount of spiritual content that they are ready for.

Typically, the performance context, for me, is that of a church mission situation and unchurched people have often been invited by friends. Perhaps they're still not that interested in spiritual issues, but they quite like their Christian neighbours, so they've agreed to come (maybe to check out if the rest of these people are OK too). All evening they've been dreading the heavy bit — where the preacher will start shouting and pointing at them. But it doesn't happen.

At the end of the show I (literally) throw out a whole load of questions; some about the plot, some about the issues, some trivial, some serious. All these are designed to say: "Discuss" to the audience. They seem visibly surprised that they've not being used for target practice. They relax. They start discussing the issues raised by the show and people actually listen to their opinions. They hear some interesting ideas. They even consider coming back!

Recently I returned to a festival where I'd performed *The Prodigal*

Grandson the previous year. At the end of this year's performance of the same show, someone approached me and said: "That show has a life of its own! I saw it here last year, and it meant something completely different to me then." I asked him why he thought this was. "I guess I was in a different place," he said.

That's the beauty of parable. God can use parables to speak to different people at different times about the issues that he knows are pertinent to them, all the time drawing people closer until they're ready to delve deeper into spiritual matters.

My hope is to set up signposts for people and to use the beauty of story and the wooing of the Holy Spirit to intrigue them as to where these signposts might lead. Certainly I don't want to be an authoritarian tour guide dragging people to places they have no interest in visiting — even if I think they should.

Or if not a signpost, then maybe a taster, something to whet their appetite for what the kingdom of God is all about. Certainly I don't want to force-feed them a full three course dinner if they're simply not hungry.

Or if not a taster, maybe an anagram, and an atmosphere where they can enjoy working out the answers. Certainly I don't want to sit there and show off with all the clever answers I've already worked out, and risk making them feel stupid.

Whichever metaphor you prefer, parables are a wonderfully effective way of communicating the Gospel. They can carry huge amounts of truth without alienating the people who don't want to be told what they should think. Parables draw people in; like with any good story, people want to know what happens next. Parables engage people; they can make people feel so much that they have to think. Parables generate discussion; they provide a genuine situation where non-Christians can express their reactions and hear our reactions.

By using parables, and by allowing space for thought and discussion we do still get to tell them what we think. But only once they've asked! The challenge then is how to engage them sufficiently with the parable and the issues it throws up for them to want to ask us. This is where we need both God's inspiration in the creative process and his Spirit to anoint it at the time it's told. This is where we need to be more like Jesus:

The gospel writer Mark tells us: *"With similar parables Jesus spoke the word to them, as much as they could understand. He did not say anything to them without using a parable. But when he was alone with his disciples he explained everything"* (Mark 4:33, 34). He intrigued the people, drew them in with his personality and his stories. The ones who wanted to hear, Jesus knew, would hear.

In the last section of the book we'll pick this up again and look more at:

1 Jesus' approach of speaking in parables and asking questions
2 What other communicators have said about this, and
3 How we may need to reassess our approach in the light of this.

We all need to be willing to look at what we're doing and be willing to let God ask us some difficult questions about it: questions like the ones I've sensed God gently repeating over the last couple of years as I've attempted to apply Jesus' model of telling stories to the people. These are some of God's questions:

Are we getting through?
Do I know the people better than you do?
Can you say different things to different people at the same time from the same story?
Who's job is it to drive it home, you or my Holy Spirit?
When do you pray more, when it's all spelled out, or when you need my Spirit to speak?
How did Jesus talk to the people?
Do you trust me?
Which do you want more; them to think, or them to know what you think?
Why do you want to put me in a box?
Will you give me more space?
Why do you bury the talents I gave you?
Did I make you to be creative or not?
Who's comments are more important, mine or your fellow Christians?
Why do you tell the people things they haven't asked?
Why won't you start where they are?
Why don't you ask me for wisdom?
Will you be more like Jesus?

Difficult questions! But I believe that God loves us enough to keep asking us these difficult questions until we are where he wants us to be.

Isn't that what all this is about? God getting us where he wants us to be. As I said earlier, this is not just about outreach, this is also about our journey toward wholeness and the proper worship of our God. Engaging our creativity in telling new stories and retelling old stories, may well revolutionise our outreach, but God knows it will almost certainly affect us deeply in the inreach and upreach departments as well. As the ancient proverb says:

Those who hear, forget.
Those who see, remember.
Those who do, understand.

By doing, we engage. It affects us. The creative process rarely leaves the creator unchanged. Which is more the theme of the next path of the journey, that of finding creative ways of telling our own story and letting that story change us further...

Our Own Stories
as Source

Our Own Stories as Source

If I can imagine nothing,
I do nothing
I choose nothing
and thereby allow my life to degenerate
from being a story
to being a mere succession of events
in a twittering world.

Dr Daniel Taylor, *The Healing Power of Stories*

This chapter changes the focus from creative ideas which have been inspired by the Bible, to those that have been born from our own journey. As Ben Okri quotes in *Birds of Heaven*:

When we have made an experience or a chaos into a story we have transformed it, made sense of it, transmuted experience, domesticated the chaos.

A significant amount of the material I've produced has been part of my response to situations and events happening to me at the time. The whole process of writing has been one of the main ways God has been able to get through to me. By following the journey through you will see how I gradually came to discover this cathartic aspect of creative writing. You'll be relieved to know that I've not included some of the more introspective material — the scripts I offer are included for use in performance and as springboards from which you can produce your own pieces.

Some of the ideas that are derived from our own story will be, by their nature, private expressions between us and God — they will be purely inreach and upreach. But, as I've said, in today's Post-modern culture people are often more interested in "Does it work?" than "Is it true?" If we are to speak in a language that people understand, then we would do well to learn how to find interesting ways to tell our stories, stories of how God has made a difference in our lives. People are increasingly open to hear our stories. They will probably balk at being told what they should do about it, but they might well be intrigued enough by your story to ask questions. Perhaps even the question: "What should I do about it?"

Non-Stop World
(1989)

A non-stop world has a non-stop mum
In a non-stop queue in a non-stop shop
And it's non-stop buying, and it's non-stop crying
'Cos it's non-stop wanting and it's just non-stop.

A non-stop world has a non-stop dad
Working non-stop hours in his non-stop job
And it's non-stop overtime for non-stop Christmas time
It's non-stop pantomime, and it's just non-stop.

A non-stop world has non-stop kids
Watching non-stop telly with their non-stop sales
Selling non-stop garbage, telling non-stop lies
In it's non-stop fashion and it's just not stopped.

A non-stop world has non-stop people
Under non-stop pressure at their non-stop parties
With their non-stop flirting and their non-stop hurting
Causing non-stop parting which will not stop.

In a non-stop world
I wish I could stop
And think
And thank
Full stop.

❏	**Principle:**	Keep it simple. Make one point per poem.
❏	**Springboard:**	What one issue keeps dominating your life?
		How would you express its dominance?

I wish I could say that this poem was written after a three day retreat at a rural monastery, but I can't. It was written on tour, in the car, rushing to the next venue. The whole poem was highly appropriate for my driven lifestyle at the time — very much a product of my own life story. I'd had the basic idea of the structure and the ending a while before, but I had been too busy to complete it. So I got the rest of the theatre company to brainstorm some ideas while we were travelling. Never waste a moment!

Blind Man's Bluff
(1989)

(To be performed by a blindfolded person walking on top of a set of chairs. The chairs are set a couple of feet apart, making it highly likely that he would fall without help. The help came from three "angels", neutrally dressed, who move the chairs according to where the character is about to step, thus keeping him safe. He /she remains oblivious to their protection throughout.)

...And I'll tell you what else. It's a good job I'm the resourceful type, 'cos I would've gone by now, off the edge, kaput, history. It's all right for you, you can see the future, all the dangers, all the problems, how things are going to work out... if they're going to work out. But I can't. What do these look like? (referring to blindfold) Where are you? A hundred feet up may not be that high to you, but these bones break. You should know that, you made them. It's all very well all this "higher way" stuff, but there's further to fall too, and more people watching you, some of them longing for you to plummet and splatter just so they can rub what's left of your nose in it and say: "I told you to take the easy way." Where are you? You say I'm special, right? Well you've got a strange way of showing it. If I'm really so special, why don't you help me? If I'm really so special, why do you leave me to cope on my own? If I'm really so special, you'd stop me from falling. The only reason I'm still up here is because I've been careful. I could go and do something really stupid, then you'd be sorry. (Nearly over-balances, an "angel" uses a chair to keep him/her on the blocks). Woah, I nearly went then, and where were you? Nowhere! It's all very well you promising there's a safety net down there, but do I know? I haven't fallen yet. No thanks to you! (freeze in antagonistic position)

⌐	**Principle:**	Use the visual to contradict the verbal.
⌐	**Springboard:**	What would you complain to God about?
		How would you contrast this visually?
		What other contrasting attitudes could you set against each other to make a point?

To digress a little, people have reminded me of this sketch nine years on, saying how it had stuck with them and how it had been a recurrent image of God's silent provision. Why did it stay in their memories for so long? I'm sure it wasn't due to any beautifully phrased sentence, but simply because it was so visual and that's how most people's memories work. Words will convey meaning and engage emotions at the time, but if we want to impact people for a long time to come, it's important to consider what visual images we are providing them with since it'll generally be the visual that will last. Those who hear, forget. Those who see, remember...

The challenge, then, is to hang the word content onto the hook of the visual so that, when the memory recalls it, the meaning will still be firmly attached. This way the Holy Spirit can take something seen months or even years before and apply it at the time the person's ready for it. It's good for all of us to ask ourselves how much do people remember from what we do? What stays with them, and why?

Of course, stories can create mental images in the minds of the listener, drawing the listener in until they can picture it in their imaginations (as radio broadcasts have proved down the years).

Do I Climb?
(1989)

Standing on the foothills of the mountain I might be.
Daunted by the ice-cap above.
Will creative juices melt the glacier of doubt?
Like a lava, scorching the ground
Leaving it fertile.
Or will the vertigo of writer's block
Stop the flow? Do I go?

Bubbling with potential
But sealed in tight with fear
Untapped and trapped by doubts
Do I climb?

I look up at me
In the distance of time
And fear, on introduction, we'll clash.
What if I'm aloof?
Too high to care about people down there.

Or cold?
Chilled by the rare atmosphere of success.
Inspiration wanes.
At pains to maintain my stride,
Do I go on?

If I leave the foothills will I ever come back
To the place that's been my home?
Could I still say "yes" to the second best views
Or stay accustomed to the custom of expecting to lose.
Can I leave it behind? And go alone?

The worry works its footholds, gives grip to doubt.
Ambition tumbles to the attrition of time.
But to bend to the pressure is to deny who I am.
Hope rumbles.

On the edge of me,
Again I count the cost,
Does it still add up?
From whichever angle I face my face —
Beside myself with fears
Below myself with tears
Behind myself, he steers the way.
I go the way I hear — up.

I climb — because I'm there.

	Principle:	The use of a metaphor for the journey of life.
	Springboard:	What image would you use for your life journey?
		How would this change if you imagined standing at the end or the beginning of your journey?

This is a clear example of the classic struggles of a writer on the journey toward finding the true self. But I'm sorry to have to tell you that I wrote this as a mick-take. That doesn't mean it's not true — not at all. It just means that I didn't realise how true it was when I wrote it!

It happened like this; I'd been attending a Writers' Circle, and they were running a poetry competition. On the penultimate week before the entries were due to be handed in, people read their offerings. I listened and felt completely alienated by it all. To me, it was all just long, posy words, which sounded "oh-so-deep-and-meaningful", but didn't mean diddly squat to me. I jokingly told my mates about it, and made the mistake of saying "I could write stuff like that." Of course, they said "Go on, then." So I had to. This is what I came up with.

It won second place! I didn't know what to do. I couldn't admit it'd all been a joke, I couldn't disappoint all those retired English teachers, now that they had a new protégé to nurture. Part of me felt completely embarrassed. Part of me was absolutely thrilled. Not that I told my mates of course!

Looking back at it now I realised that, sadly, the only way I could have ever allowed myself to write something approaching serious poetry, was to take the mick. Such was the culture of laddishness we had developed that I would never have had the freedom to write like that seriously. It would've been impossible. But without realising it, by doing it as a joke, I had lowered the stakes. Unwittingly I'd tripped over a way to allow me the chance to give it a go. And it flowed! And I really enjoyed writing it. By doing it as a stunt, there was no tension, no fear of failure, no self consciousness, and it all came quite easily. How much of our creativity do we feel we have to hide from people around us who, we feel, wouldn't understand?

One of the reasons why I've included the previous three pieces is that they sum up where I was at the time — driven by busyness, angry at God's apparent distance and unable to be myself. All this while working full-time in an evangelistic team! These frustrations built over the next months and years, I became more irritable and difficult to be with and then in May 1991 my wife left me. It was devastating. I tried everything to save the marriage, but she had lost all hope and I had to face the fact that there wasn't going to be a reconciliation.

I share this not to be dramatic, or to engender sympathy. But knowing this will both inform your reading of the material and help you understand the role creative writing was to have in God speaking to me and healing me.

For about a year I didn't write or perform at all. I was convinced that it was precisely the pressured, itinerant lifestyle that had sucked me into this black hole of insecurity and low self esteem which had, in turn, driven my wife from me. Gently, gradually, God brought me to see that being in front of an audience had indeed exacerbated the problems, but that the need for affirmation and security had always been there and now was the time to face it and deal with it.

A traumatic year later, I was beginning to take a few faltering steps back onto the stage. Then a friend asked me the simple question: "Are you writing?"

I wasn't. But I began to. I sat at my computer and wrote for at least a couple of hours each day. The taps at the end of my fingers had been opened and so much stuff gushed out. Most of it was muddied, a lot of it was toxic, but some of it was pure 'living water'. All of it was the most ME I'd ever allowed myself to be on paper. For the first time I had no audience to write for. For the first time I was free from the pressure of second guessing what an audience might think of me; free from having to say the right thing; and free to discover what I really felt about things. I had discovered my very own unexcavated diamond shaft which, if I chose to, was mine to mine.

Joint Cell
(May 1992)

(Handcuffed to an invisible person, trying to communicate with them)

Talk to me! This is driving me scatty. What is this? Some vow of silence? Face it. We're stuck with each other.

What do you think these handcuffs are, bracelets? (Moves suddenly) How d'you ignore me when I nearly wrench your arm from its socket? (Tugs at arm again) Don't you feel that? (Calming down) I know I lose control, but you just sitting there sends me... (Struggles for word). You... Me... Handcuffs... Cell... That's all there is. And you don't even talk to the walls!

(More to self) Ironic thing is, I'm a good listener. Always have been. (To partner) But you wouldn't know that, you've only heard me rant and scream at you. Go on, try me. Talk to me!

Do you think it does any good? Staring at the wall all day? Or don't you want it to, right, you don't want it to do you? This is you beating yourself isn't it?

I know you resent me being here. I know you hate everything about me. But does ignoring me really help? Let's assume we did talk. Even if you still hated me, at least you'd know what made me tick. Would that be such a loss?

Or is this a pride thing? Is this you trying to prove something to yourself or what? (Realisation) Right, talking to me means you fail because you admit I'm here, yes? You opening your mouth doesn't make me suddenly appear. Shutting your mouth hasn't made me disappear has it? You're stuck with me. You won't get rid of me 'til you're let out. I'm here, it's real, do you think these cuts on your wrist are just a rash or what? It's real, it's happening and the sooner you come to terms with it, the sooner we can both start surviving. You can't hide in an eight by five foot cell.

Oh, but then of course you can if the other person's not actually there, can't you? And I'm not am I? Don't answer that, there's no point, 'cos no one actually asked it, did they? Don't answer that either, just testing. But then I'm not likely to catch you out, because you *know* there's no one else here, just you, on your own, nobody else. I certainly couldn't catch you out even if I did exist, could I? No, no, you're far too clever, you've thought it all through. You know that if you ignore something for long enough, where does it go? I'll answer that, don't worry. "Away", that's where it goes, it goes "away". You worked that out long ago, along with "my eyes are closed so no one can see me" and "it's dark so someone's packed away the countryside for the night". Come on, ostrich-brain. Talk to me!

Just think about it will you? And let me know. I won't be far away.

| **Principle:** | Allow a concept to become a person and allow this person to speak to you. |
| **Springboard:** | Which concept is currently having a big impact on your life? What would he or she say to you? Would you answer back? How? |

Whose voice is doing the talking? It's not an actual person, it's a concept, or actually a personification of a concept. By setting up the image of me being trapped in a small prison cell with a personification of pain, I had allowed myself to face my pain and converse with "him".

In terms of inreach and upreach, splurging all this onto the screen was so good for me. Until this point I'd never really been able to be honest with God about what was going on. At times it felt as if I was screaming on the inside and not able to let it out. But the writing process allowed me to get it out, not in a self-indulgent or introspective way, but with a strong sense of God looking over my shoulder as I wrote, enabling me to give these emotions up to him and receive his peace in exchange.

But this does not mean that we should show other people every angst-ridden lament we ever write. Sometimes ideas will come which are suitable to pass on to others (as I've done here). Other times the ideas are best kept between you and God (I've many private scribbles in my notebooks which no one is likely to see). I consider these as private letters, written directly to God. Naturally some of these letters will also be suitable to turn into memos for more general distribution. But many won't, and these are just as important (if not more so) than the ones you allow other people to read.

Strangely, the more private you make it, the more safe you'll probably feel, the more honest you'll be, and so the more likely you'll be to produce something True. By freeing ourselves from the expectations of any audience other than God, we provide our imaginations with the conditions in which they can be fertile and so we're more likely to produce work that will relate to others. The problem is that this means that you're still tempted to be looking for ideas for general consumption, rather than just being with God. I've still not found a way out of this conundrum, but at least I know it's there. So does God, thankfully!

Job Satisfaction
(May 1992)

A while back someone I know had a job he absolutely adored. This job was great. This job made him really happy and, in the right sense, proud. But one day someone confronted him: "It's no wonder you love your job, because your job's too safe, too cushioned, too comfortable — there are so many perks attached you've probably forgotten what your job is really like". And he challenged him to find out. He dared him to remove all the perks: "Find out why you're so proud, take your job right down to the very core, and find out what your job's really like."

So he did. Because he wanted to know. He stripped away everything that was comfortable, all the benefits that had accrued in the years that he'd been with his job. And it's only fair to say that, for a while, things were hard, after all, it was a dangerous thing to risk. This new job — the change was that drastic — this new job could have really disappointed, could've really turned sour on him. He had to face the possibility that it might have been true; that he might have only loved his job because of all the perks.

For a while things seemed to be in the balance, but gradually the true nature of his job emerged, and he said to the one who challenged him "You see, my job is exactly what I want. In fact, by taking all the luxuries away, my job has become even better; refined, refocused, don't you think?" "Yes," he admitted, "Your job is great, your job is all anyone could ask for."

And so my friend was even more proud of his job than before. He couldn't stop talking about him... It. Sorry. He couldn't stop talking about it. No, it is "him", in the script it says "him", I'm sure it does. Hang on a second. (Checks script) It is "him", but a job is an "it" not a "him", uh, sorry, I've messed it up, it is a "him", and it's a capital J. So it's not a "job" it's Job, and "he" has a capital H. Sorry, I'll do it again for you.

(Return to start, and on second run through:)
...And so my friend was even more proud of His Job than before. He couldn't stop talking about him. And He looked forward to many more years of enjoying His Job.

☐	**Principle:**	The same text can have more than one meaning.
☐	**Springboard:**	What other misunderstandings (cross-purposes) have you observed? How could you develop this double meaning?

A strange one to read, especially toward the end. I envisage it as being read by the actor, who then realises he/she's got it wrong. Although, I've deliberately left the Js and the Hs in lower case letters, to allow you (hopefully) to enjoy the Aha! moment of realisation in the same way as the audience would. It could also be performed by an actor having learnt it, but then in the act of performing, notices the mistake, checks the script and then goes back to the start and does it again with the correct meaning. It does need this second run through, so that the audience can listen to the same words, now with the intended meaning, rather than being frustrated at having missed it on the first hearing.

This piece could also have been included in the category of material inspired by the Bible. But the motivation for writing it came very much from my own situation and my hope that, like Job, I was being refined. The line "For a while things seemed to be in the balance" was precisely where I felt I was at the time, and I suspect that writing this piece played a large part in bringing me through.

No One Knows Now
(June 1992)

(Best performed with a small but decent cassette player as a prop. Actually pressing the *FF*, *Rew*, *Play* and *Stop* buttons at the appropriate points. As to what is on the tape when *Play* is pressed; the obvious choice seemed to be a recording of "Be still and know that I am God", but then why go for the obvious? It can also be performed as a voice-over for an appropriate video, which is similarly cued to fit with the poem.)

I can press fast forward (press *FF*)
Flee far into my future
Not knowing now
But knowing how
Things are bound to be better by then.

I can press rewind (press *Rew*)
Retrace tracks far behind
Still not knowing now
But knowing how
I'd walk differently if the tracks came round again.

I can press play (press *Play* – we hear a pre-recorded singing of "Be still and know that I am God" repeated several times)
My best game's (hide behind cassette player)
Hide and seek
Still not knowing now
But knowing how
When teacher blows her whistle
And play time ends
I'll be left
Still hiding
From friends.

Or I can press stop (press *Stop*)
Be still and know now.
Because no one knows now, now.

And then, once I've stopped,
I'm ready to press play again.
(press *Play*, which will continue to play the same song repeating).

❏	**Principle:**	Take an everyday object as a metaphor.
❏	**Springboard:**	Play the game "This object reminds me of life or God or me because…"

I was pressing stop quite a lot at this time and, to take the metaphor further, I was also pressing record. Two months into this new-found approach to writing I realised that I was onto something. Writing was proving to be a real lifeline. My notebooks were filling up at quite a rate. They were a form of diary or journal. Not the "Today I posted a letter" type of diary, but somewhere private I could go and be honest with myself and with God. Somewhere I could splurge ideas, frustrations, desires, observations and images. Somewhere I could pray in a way that was more real than I was used to. But the most significant change was that I was just writing for me and God. All the pressure of "I have to produce a sketch on…" had been turned on its head. Now it had become "This is an issue for me at the moment, and this is how I can express it."

In January 1993, on a whim of an idea, I began writing a fictional dialogue between me and my ex-wife. From the start, the whole idea took on a life of its own; my imagination was free to say the things I felt needed to be said. Each day I'd come back from mime school and write for hours. I didn't structure it, so I had no idea what would happen next. But I knew that if I kept writing, I'd find out. It was remarkable. I splurged onto the screen and as I read it back to myself I learned so much about me and the situation. At one point, I distinctly remember reading words from the screen and, like a divine electric shock, it hit me: "That's it! That's the problem! I don't like myself!"

It's incredible to think that I hadn't realised this before. God used my own words to get through to me. The process of writing was the key which unlocked so much of my past pain, and because he was always there at my shoulder — reading, comforting, holding me as I wrote — it was so healing. I'm so grateful to God for the tools of creativity which he's given me, they've probably been the main way in which God and I have been able to connect.

This was inreach and upreach as I'd never known it before. Whether or not these scripts would ever be used in outreach was a secondary issue for me — I was getting to know me and God in an entirely new way. And without being aware of it, I was also learning to write.

Making Bad Things Go Away
(December 1992)

Pronounce G as in Gnome — no sound.
Pronounce U as in Guilt — still no sound.
Pronounce N as in Autumn — still no sound.
So, with a G and a U and an N all silent
We can get the word GUN to go.
Take S as in Island
And GUNS are all gone.

Pronounce W as in wreck
A as in Death
We've got N as in Autumn
Then take T as Castle or Crochet
If we say it this way then W. A. N. T. WANT goes away.

Take C from Scissors, and your mother was right;
There's no such word as CAN'T
Take K as in Knock, I as in Friend,
And L as in Calm, and KILL has to end.

So, we've got rid of GUNS and WANT and TAKING and KILLING
Add P from Receipt and you mop up any SPILLING.
By simply speaking it away.
Or "Say it away" as I like to say.

Take O from Foetus and WOE has to go.
Take E from Aerobics and H from Ghost
And HATE takes a one-way ticket to the coast.
Take B as in Doubt
And BEATINGS lose out.
Take R from Iron, and the first D from Wednesday
And we can delete 18 silent letters
And make bad things go away.

Now, we can say:
Ta-ta to TERROR, shut up to SHOUT
Au revoir to ERROR, and get out to DOUBT
We can bundle up a bagful of BUTS.

We can do away with DIRT, say skidaddle to SCANDAL
Hit out at HURT, and victimise VANDAL.
Tell GORE "no more", wipe out WAR
Pay off the POOR, show PAIN the door.
Tell LUST to get lost, make GREED count the cost.
Give HORROR scope to predict its own demise
Let scholars cope with the letting go of LIES.
Make sure that DISEASE gets wise
And curls up in the corner and dies.

We can make these bad things go away.
We just have to announce
How to pronounce
These words
The silent way.
We can make these words go away.
Unless anyone else knows a better way?

| | **Principle:** | Propose a completely ludicrous idea as a discussion starter or as a set up to providing a feasible idea. |
| | **Springboard:** | How would you propose to get rid of pain or disease or greed? |

If only it was that easy! Meanwhile, back in the real world:

Insanity
(March 1993)

A friend of mine is a well known psychologist.
Well, he's a psychologist I know well.

This well known psychologist said to me:
"Insanity is being out of touch with the real world."
And he says things like:
"Insanity is being out of touch with the real world" quite often.
And when he says things like:
"Insanity is being out of touch with the real world."
He begins them by saying:
"A friend of mine who's a well-known psychologist says"
And then says what he wants to say,
Like: "Insanity is being out of touch with the real world."

And he does this quite often.
And he can.
Because it's true — he knows himself better than anyone.

Unless, of course, he's insane
And out of touch with the real world.

❑	**Principle:**	Poems are everywhere just waiting to be found and formed.
❑	**Springboard:**	What memorable things have been said to you? Use these as a starting point or end point of a story or dialogue or poem.

This is true. My friend does this, and he gets away with it! But I knew this for a long time before it occurred to me that it could be a poem. I knew that the process of writing this situation up into a poem consolidated the impact of his ideas on my life.

Another piece that happened at this time has already been referred to in the section on using the Bible as a source. This is the original version of the idea on page 59. It is more personal, referring to my situation which, as you'll see, was a dangerous one.

Counting Backwards From Ten
(March 1993)

Thou shalt not covet thy neighbour's wife.

Thou shalt not bear false witness against thy neighbour, neither shalt thou have the need therof for thou hast not coveted thy neighbour's wife.

Thou shalt not steal. Thou shalt not steal thy neighbour's faith in his wife. Neither, verily, shalt thou steal thy neighbour's wife by committing adultery with her.

Thou shalt not kill. Thou shalt not put to the sword the unit of the family, for thou hast not stolen thy neighbour's faith in his wife by committing adultery with her, for thou hast not borne false witness against him, nor had the need therof for thou hast not coveted thy neighbour's wife.

Thou shalt honour thy father and thy mother. Verily, thou shalt honour thy father and thy mother since thou hast not put to the sword the unit of the family, for thou hast not stolen thy neighbour's faith in his wife by committing adultery with her, for thou hast not borne false witness against him, nor had the need therof for thou hast not coveted thy neighbour's wife.

Thou shalt remember the Sabbath day and keep it holy, and thereby bring greater honour to thy father and thy mother whom thou hast not dishonoured by putting to the sword the unit of the family, for thou hast not stolen thy neighbour's faith in his wife by committing adultery with her, for thou hast not borne false witness against him, nor had the need therof for thou hast not coveted thy neighbour's wife.

Thou shalt not take the name of the Lord in vain. For thou hast not forgotten the Sabbath day and have kept it holy by not bringing dishonour to thy father and thy mother whom thou hast not dishonoured by putting to the sword the unit of the family, for thou hast not stolen thy neighbour's faith in his wife by committing adultery with her, for thou hast not borne false witness against him, nor had the need therof for thou hast not coveted thy neighbour's wife.

Thou shalt not bow down to any graven images, for thou shalt have no other gods before me, for thou shalt love the Lord thy God with all thy heart, and with all thy soul, and with all thy mind, and with all thy strength, and thou shalt love thy neighbour as thy self, which shall be a gtreat love, since thou canst now love thy self greatly, since thou hast done these things, nor hast thou the need thereof, since thou hast loved the Lord thy God.

Thou shalt not. Thou shalt not. For the promises of God are Yea and Amen.

⌐	**Principle:**	Use a familiar text and put your story into it.
⌐	**Springboard:**	Which commandment is The Big One for you at the moment?
		How would you restructure the list to portray this?

Writing and reciting this poem strenthened my resolve in a dangerous situation. What I didn't know was that all this writing was God's way of preparing me for the difficult times ahead. The crisis of the separation had come, but I knew there was still the divorce proceedings to face. Two years of gradual healing had passed, but it wasn't all blue skies yet — there was still a bank of black clouds up ahead that could not be avoided. I knew this, I just didn't expect the thunder to be quite so loud!

As the two year anniversary of our split approached, the pressure built — would she file for divorce as she'd said she would, or was there still hope? I got more and more tense. I was finding normal tasks like climbing the stairs exhausting. I was so twitchy that I could hardly hold a normal conversation, I couldn't focus on anything that required any concentration. Writing the next monologue was not an academic exercise in constructing a piece about a breakdown! It was happening, and I needed to get in touch with it. From all that I'd learned from writing before, splurging it onto paper seemed the only way to deal with it.

Concentration Span
(May 1993)

My concentration span doesn't last very long time ago in a far away land there must be some way out of here today gone tomorrow is another day in day out of bounds up to you with so much to say if only I could keep my train of thought my concentration span doesn't seem to be or not to be that is the question of time before it all falls around my feat of great strength of mind if I use your toilet humour me please I really find it very difficult to stay on the same subject to satisfactory references to my past life Jim but not as we know too much already greeny sort of colour me beautiful morning has broken and beyond reasonable repair off into two's everyone and find a space to find myself and get my thinking straight down the line of thought I was doing OK I thought my concentration span of a man's hand is better that a bird in the bush backwards in coming forward by the Bishop of Bath and Wells up and before you know it you're crying like a baby milk it for all it's worth trying to concentrated orange juice, to concentrate on one thing at a time to get a grip on yourself abuse of my basic human rights and wrongs I don't claim to understand up and scream enough is enough to be going on with for now and again on the swings you lose on the roundabout forty two I would guess but he has gone grey early bird catches the worm your way out of that one rule for you can't be too careful I say I say I say when is a door not a door? when it's a jar of raspberry jam tailing back 6 miles on the M25 clockwise after the event of the year dot dot dot dash dash dash it all I want for Christmas is my two front teeth under my pillow to rest my head aches and pains in the neck of the wood if I could but I can't help myself and make myself at home sweet home is where the heart is deceitful above all things to do people to see deadlines to meet you in the foyer at eight that far too quickly does it make sense of despair any loose change in the weather people like me. Would you mind if I had a break... down?

❏   **Principle:**   Take an observation to an extreme to create an impact.
❏ **Springboard:**   What crisis situations have you gone through?
                         How could you express this in creative ways?
                         Do you feel you need to?

This piece was to become the climax of the *People Like Me* show that I started putting together a year later. The show deals with a performer's increasingly desperate attempts to get his audience to like him. Eventually, after trying every style of performance he can think of, he's still convinced that (despite their applause) they don't like him, and he cracks up. But before I performed it I had to go through it.

Harness The Darkness
(October 1993)

"Keep me safe and bring me home"
– saves such a weighty, wordy tome of pleas.
Please, blow your breeze of benevolent ease
And raise me gently from my knees
– of beggar not of prayer –
And be there, while I'm getting there.

Unfold my furrowed forehead
With stories told by borrowed bed.
May your lullaby obey
And hush away the dread of dreadful dreams.
Bring your beams of night-light to my sight
And deem that despite the plight
And for all the fear
Your face will always stay this clear.

Instruct this dark drug "Destruct"
That he has served to reconstruct my life.
That you allowed his cloud to shroud
But, having done his worst,
He saw you drive the hearse away,
And I heard him curse the resurrection day.
Today, let 'Destruct' deduct
That you are still the lover of my soul.
You undertook to undertake, and let him break
That bowl of thirty years of fears,
It broke and dyed my vision red.
Yet bloodshed should bed
The bulbs of conquered dread,
And bloodshed will wed
My hungry heart and angry head.

Channel this wild white-water energy,
Newly born beneath and breaking free,
Damn the dam that damaged me
And drown the downward sucking sea.

Harness the darkness,
And have it hum the hymns of how to cope.
Saddle the sadness,
So I sit astride the kaleidoscope of hope
And ride; with teeth full of grit and bridle bit,
Wide-eyed and knowing why I died.

❏	**Principle:**	Prayer need not always be spontaneous.
		Sometimes careful selection of the right words can help.
❏	**Springboard:**	How would you phrase the core cry of your heart?

Despite what people say about quoting your own work, I mumbled some, or all, of this to myself most days during this period. There was a real sense of anticipation about what God had up his sleeve, and given that God was a lot bigger and/or a lot closer than he used to be, I was almost excited.

But bruises were still healing and when someone pokes you in a sensitive part, you react. One such prod happened in church with the speaker going on as if being a Christian meant you sailed through life problem free. This was my reaction:

Your Woodginess
(March 1994)

Oh Lord, we worship your woodginess.
For you are the Forever Fluffy One,
The All Squidgy, Squiggly One.
And we giggle and gush in your presence
As we raise our hoorays all the days of our trouble-free lives.
For we are your simple dimples.
And we trust in the warmth of your cuteness everlasting.
And we declare that you are beyond all naughtiness,
Above all itchy twitchiness,
And higher than all horridness.
And we raise our hippity hip hop hoorays all the days of our trouble-free lives.
And we want to be your best friends.
And we want to give you all our sweeties,
Even the blackcurrant ones
Because we think you are... just... so... nice.

	Principle:	Use of satire can be a powerful tool in helping people to laugh at themselves.
	Springboard:	What aspect of "religion" do you feel needs knocking down? How can humour help you do this?

Writing this was a better option than standing up and screaming! As I scribbled away in my notebook, people in the pews around me probably thought I was being spiritual, diligently taking notes on the sermon. A couple of weeks later, I showed *Woodginess* to a friend, and she challenged me to write an alternative version, an "antidote" if you like. Far from being a writing exercise, it became genuine upreach.

Your Woundedness
(April 1994)

Oh Lord, we worship your woundedness.
For you are the All Forlorn One,
The Venerable Vulnerable One.
Yet we wriggle and rush in your presence
And we raise our gaze some of the days of our trouble-filled lives.
For we are your stuttering servants.

And we struggle to trust in the rumours of your rootedness.
And we are intrigued by you.
You who are beyond all banality,
Above all that is oral,
And higher than all hyperbole.
And we raise our squinting, short-sighted gaze
Some of the days of our trouble-filled lives.
And we want you to be our best friend.
And we want to give you all our weakness,
Even the weakness that doesn't let us doubt.
Because we think you are... just... so... so...

I'll be honest, there were certain aspects of church life which I was wasn't so enamoured with. At times I struggled with some of the culture. Some of this was due to me still being in a sensitive state. All the same, it did me good to get it out. Laughing at ourselves can be a wonderful release.

Some Days
(May 1994)

Some days – dandruff
Some days – a liberated scalp

Some days – too lazy to shave
Some days – designer stubble

Some days – my heart's a mass of crumbling rock
Some days – it's star dust

Some days – lonely
Some days – free

Some days – moody
Some days – being true to me

Some days – it's the end of the world
Some days – Jesus is coming back.

❑ **Principle:**	A structure need not be complex.
❑ **Springboard:**	Do you change?
	What are your contrasting attitudes to certain days?

I change! Not just during the storms, but even on smoother seas. It's part of the way I'm made. The only difference was that by this time, instead of instantly accusing myself of gross and deliberate sin, I was starting to accept my mood swings as part of who I am.

My church upbringing had drummed into me that I must be "a faithful brother". This meant that I had to be the same, strong, reliable person every week. I saw very few examples of people admitting they had "off days", and certainly never from the pulpit. There was very little weakness or vulnerability shown so I assumed that this just wasn't allowed if you were going to be a Proper Christian. There are large parts of my church upbringing that I'm incredibly grateful for. This wasn't one of them!

Now I'm hoping to become "a faithful brother" in a new sense — that of, being faithful to who God made me, and how far he's brought me along the journey toward becoming fully human. When I get to heaven he's not going to say to me: "Why weren't you more like... (whoever)?", but he might well say: "Why weren't you more like you?" He's made us with everything we need for what we're supposed to do, and he wants us to be fully "us" — with our own unique stories to tell.

At this point I was toying with the idea of telling my story in the form of a show. But I knew that sometimes when you're honest about how God has helped you deal with pain, people can accuse you of using him as a crutch. As it happens very few have, but I'm glad that I risked it. I came to the decision that I'd rather be honest and risk their derision, than deny what had been happening. After all, if you've got a broken leg, a crutch can be pretty handy.

Both Ways (The Poem)
(June 1994)

Things go wrong
And fists shake
And necks ache
As we take out our pain
And fling it up again in the face of the Faithful One saying
"Why did you let this happen?"

And when in a while he gives us a glimpse of his answer
When he shows us a life once crushed by pain
That has since known his touch

We sneer again
And call him a crutch.

❏	**Principle:**	A single point can be adapted into poem form.
❏	**Springboard:**	What points have you used or heard recently which could be expressed in a different form?

Ideas can often take on different forms. This idea was later adapted into a two person sketch:

Both Ways (The Sketch)

(The whole sketch to be performed off-stage, as if the actors have forgotten to turn their radio mics off.)

1	And where's my brush?
2	You left it in the dressing room.
1	No it does, it really annoys me.
2	I know.
1	I'm angry. I'm sorry, but I am. I'm just angry.
2	No, don't be sorry.
1	Can I borrow yours then?
2	It's good to be angry about it.
1	It's just not fair.
2	I know. Don't get gel on it though.
1	Doesn't he hear them or what? Can't he hear them screaming up at him?
2	Of course he hears them. Is this my script or yours?
1	But he doesn't do anything about it. I mean, how do you turn a deaf ear to cries like that?
2	No, this one smells of tobacco.
1	Has he no idea?
2	Of course he does.
1	Doesn't he see their poverty?
2	Of course he does.
1	Doesn't he see how it crushes their humanity?
2	And it crushes him.
1	So how can he turn a blind eye to it? I mean he calls himself a God of justice and yet he lets people shout at him like that.
2	So we're rehearsing Thursday, yeah?

1	What sort of justice is it to let them get away with that? It's farcical. There they are, with their fists waving away: "If you're a God of love why don't you do something about all this suffering?" It's farcical!
2	And that's the "God is..." sketch.
1	They blame him for all the suffering. But do they give him any credit for all the beautiful things they see every single day of the week, like bolero they do. No, but the second anything goes wrong they're out there shaking their fists at him. It's pathetic.
2	Flies are undone, Rob.
1	What? Uh, thanks. They can't have it both ways, they just can't have it both ways.
2	But they don't see that that's what they're doing.
1	No, I know they don't. I'm just angry. I'm sorry, but I am. I'm just angry.
2	We need to work out what we're going to wear for the Adam and Eve sketch.
1	Doesn't he see their poverty? Doesn't he see how it crushes their humanity?
2	Yes, he does.
1	But he does nothing about it.
2	Yes he does. I mean you know he does. All you've been through.
1	Yeah, but when I try to tell them...
2	Yes, but...
1	When I get a word in.
2	But...
1	When they stop ranting away "If you're a God of love, why don't you do something about all this suffering?" I try to tell them, how God has been with me in my pain, my dark times, how he's been there in my suffering, that he does "do something". And you know what they call him?
2	They call him "a crutch".
1	Exactly. "In a world of suffering, how can you believe in a God of love?" Well it's a good job for them, that you can.
2	Rob, is your radio mic on?
1	Rats!

❑	**Principle:**	A single point can become dialogue by discussing it.
❑	**Springboard:**	Take an idea you're used to using and translate it into a different form of communication.

As you can see — the same idea in a different form. A little while after this I had to knock together something for an evening looking at the issue of suffering. There had been a last minute panic, due to someone having to drop out of the programme so we were left with some gaps. I decided to experiment, to see whether this same idea could work in a different form again: I went up on stage with my banjo and spoke in my best disaffected singer/songwriter intro voice.

Both Ways (The Song)

Singer	You know, it makes me angry — when things go wrong in someone's life, people shout at God: "Why don't you do something?" And when he does, and sorts out someone's life, the same people call him a crutch. So I've written a song, and it's called (much quicker) *You know, it makes me angry — when things go wrong in someone's life, people shout at God "Why don't you do something?" And when he does, and sorts out someone's life, the same people call him a crutch.* It goes something like this (to music):
(Sings)	You know It makes me angry That when things go wrong in someone's life People shout at God "Why don't you do something?" And when he does Sort out someone's life The same people The very same people Exactly the same people Call him a Call him a Call him a crutch.
(Speaking)	That's the title track off my new album, called *You Know...* Yeah, you know.

> ❏ **Principle:**   A single point can become a song lyric.
> ❏ **Springboard:**   What other form of communication could
>   this idea become?

To be honest, it didn't really work that well, but I'm sure that was because I was under-rehearsed. The reason I include it is to show the possibilities of different uses of any one idea. In whatever form, this idea was part of the result of me considering whether to tell my story, how to tell my story and how people would react if I did. I was about to take the plunge.

People Like Me
(July 1994)

(An hour long solo show — too long to script, you'll just have to see it. Or buy the video!)

> ❏ **Principle:**   Be honest.
> ❏ **Springboard:**   What's the central issue that you've had to let God
>   deal with in your life?
>   How could you communicate this in a creative way?

Quite a while before, I'd scribbled in a notebook: "Lord, melt my pen if I write what I don't know." It never graduated to a higher form, but it still had a great impact on me. So when I felt ready to put a whole show together I wanted it to be about the issues God had been dealing with. At this point, all I could really say was how God had begun to heal me of my low self-esteem, and free me from my driven, desperate need for affirmation. I wanted to express what God was teaching me about his unconditional love: how he didn't just love me, but he liked me too, and that there was nothing I could do to make him like me more. Or less. I also wanted to state my gratitude to those people who had "been Jesus to me" through the dark times. I wanted to tell my story.

So I constructed a character who went through a whole list of different styles of performance in his search for affirmation from the audience. Eventually the character gets to the end of his energy and breaks down on stage. From here I step out of the performance and admit that the character was me and chat for a short while about how God's unconditional love and the love of Christian friends had brought me to a place of far greater security and self esteem.

The first time I performed the *People Like Me* show was a great test for me (apart from all the normal first night nerves and my first attempt at a full solo show). What if they didn't like it? Would I cope with the rejection? Would it crush me? Would I be able to distinguish between what they thought of the show and what they thought of me? As it happened they loved the show. But it was good for me to risk it.

I was amazed by how many people related to what I'd portrayed; how many people struggled with the same issues. Some hadn't had to go as far under before beginning to deal with it, others had gone further and were still coming back up, but so many people knew that what I was trying to portray was true. Many of those who came up to me after the show communicated a sense of relief that there were other people who had the same struggles. I was touched. But I wouldn't have discovered this unless I'd taken the risk, been honest and told my story "warts and all". Another way to put it would be as follows.

The Wood Chopper
(March 1998)

There once was a master wood chopper. He had such style, flare and charisma. Over the years he'd developed wonderfully complex routines to wow his audience — throws, twirls, catches, spins. People came from miles to watch him chop wood.

His *Wonderful Wood Chopping Show* was a resounding success and his manager encouraged him: "Throw the axe higher, spin it a third time, delay the catch just a split second longer — they'll love it." Then one day, in the middle of his most complex routine, he misjudged a behind-the-back-throw and the blade of the axe came down on the palm of his hand. The crowd gasped, he saw blood, but such was the adrenaline that he felt no pain. He carried on, and the crowd were convinced it was just a trick.

Back in the dressing room his manager said "Did you hear the gasp, and the roar when you carried on? We'll blunt the blade. We'll use blood capsules. They'll love it." The wood chopper agreed and even more people flooded to see the act. Occasionally, he mis-timed the catch, but the audience couldn't distinguish between real blood and stage blood, and the cuts soon healed. It was worth it — ticket sales were soaring.

But after a while, they wanted more. They wanted higher throws, more twirls, more spins, more danger. The more he gave them, the more times he cut his hands. The more he cut his hands the more pain he had performing. The more pain he had performing, the more distractions, the more mistakes, the more cuts, more pain, more mistakes, more cuts, pain, mistakes, cuts, pain, mistakes, cuts... until he knew he had to stop. No one else knew. He kept his hands well bandaged off stage, and they moved too fast to see on stage, but he knew.

"Throw it higher," said his manager. "They want more, and you've got to give them more." He gave them more — more height, more speed, more pain, more mistakes, more cuts, more pain. They still wanted more. More height, more speed, more pain, more mistakes, more danger. More!! More height, more speed, more pain, more mistakes, more cuts, more pressure, more cuts, more height, more pain, more height, more pain, more height... and as the axe spun down, he knew he had to stop, he turned his hand palm down, and watched the axe hit the back of his wrist separating the hand from the rest of his body.

The crowd saw the hand, motionless, and separated from the arm. They saw its colour which had spread almost to the wrist, and they knew he'd had no choice. The hand had turned gangrenous. He'd chopped it off just in time to save his life.

❏   **Principle:**   Take one symbol (here, the axe) and tell your
                         story using it.
❏ **Springboard:**   What symbol would you choose to represent your life?

Horrible, isn't it? I really tried to give the story a happy ending. But it just wouldn't be forced. Part of me wanted to bring in a "Jesus figure" who would heal the hand and call him back into using his skills again — since that's what has happened in my own story. But it was too cheesy. So I left it there. A warning. A call to be vigilant with my motives. In real life Jesus has healed me and allowed me a second chance to use my skills in a more whole and healthy way. But leaving the story at this point has more of an impact on me. It reminds me of what might have happened. It makes me grateful for what did happen.

Conclusion

There's a wonderful scene in the film about C.S. Lewis' marriage, *Shadowlands*, where he asks a student "Why do we read?" I don't remember the student's answer, but I remember Lewis': "We read to know we're not alone." If we tell our stories honestly, people will almost certainly identify with us, because many of the things we go through are common to all. They'll know that they're not alone. But if we only say what we should be like, and exhort others to try harder, if we forget to mention that we also fail, then we only convince people that we're really sorted and that they're very much alone in their struggles. By telling our stories, admitting our struggles and shortcomings, and saying how God helps us through them, we help each other to know that we're not alone.

By finding creative ways of telling our stories we can communicate the Gospel to people in a language they can relate to and understand. The impact of a true life story can be very strong, especially in today's Post-modern society where, as has been said, people are more interested in the question "Does your faith work?" than in the question "Is your faith true?"

But as you've seen, some of the material in this section wasn't written to persuade people that my faith works. It was written as part of the process of grappling with life, faith and meaning. Being creative in this way has been so crucial in getting to grips with these issues and with God. So much of the progress I've made has been possible because God has entered into the cathartic effect of creativity. God will, when allowed, transform what is potentially just indulgent introspection into a wonderful process of inreach and upreach. He'll work his healing, wholeness and beauty into what otherwise would be a depressing and painful situation. The following image has helped me understand this process:

> The artist finds a screwed-up piece of paper discarded in the corner of his studio. He opens the paper out and finds a labyrinth of creases. He tries to make the paper as flat as possible, but he knows the creases will never completely disappear. So rather than trying, he decides to let the creases inspire him to create something from the paper as it is. He works with the lines and angles that are now built into the paper and finds shapes and images in the creases. He shades them, he colours them, he adds lines, he underlines lines, he works and works until he's thrilled with what he's made. Then he frames the picture and hangs it

in his gallery where he proudly shows his guests what he made from a crushed, screwed-up piece of discarded paper.

This simple image encapsulates the fall, redeption, sanctification, and glorification, and portrays the central theme of this chapter: that God honours our pain and changes us through it.

> In Italy for 30 years under the Borgias they had warfare, terror, murder, bloodshed they produced Michelangelo, Leonardo de Vinci and the Renaissance. In Switzerland they had brotherly love, 500 years of democracy and peace, and what did they produce? The cuckoo clock.
>
> Graham Green, *The Third Man*

These are some of the questions I felt God asking me as I travelled along this path of the journey:

> Are you "getting through" to me?
> Why aren't you real with me?
> Do you think I can handle your honesty?
> Will I like you less if you scribbled something inappropriate?
> Don't I know the real you already?
> Did I inspire the Psalms, Lamentations, Job?
> Why do you run away from your struggles?
> Have I given you all you need to express yourself?
> Will I be with you as you face your struggles?
> Will you be more you?
> Why did I invent church?
> Aren't you bored with just saying "the right thing"?
> Have I given you people you can be real with?
> Will you risk telling others how you feel?
> Will you use your own voice?
> Why do you want to hide what I've done in you?
> Do you tell your story so they'll think you're great, or I'm great?

In the next chapter we'll take this further. We'll consider the cathartic role of creativity in dealing with our response to other people's situations. We had a fascinating example of this in 1997 with people's responses to the death of Diana, Princess of Wales. Why did so many queue up to write messages in those books? Surely people realised that they were unlikely to be read by anyone. But it didn't matter.

These expressions of grief were written primarily for the benefit of the person writing them. It was an important part of dealing with the grief. But it wasn't only these messages. Recently I was in a bookshop, picking my way through the bargain bucket, and I found a book entitled *Sun Readers' Poems at the Death of Diana*. People again needed to put pen to paper to deal with their grief.

In addition to the role of creativity in our response to other peoples' stories, we'll also look at creative ways of telling other peoples' stories. How can we draw people in? How can we use the vehicle of someone's story to convey a message?

Other People's
Stories as Source

Other People's Stories as Source

When the hearing and telling of stories captures our imaginations, it enables us at the deepest level to take our lives seriously. By envisioning other worlds, we become more capable of listening to God and to ourselves, and of growing in God's image.

Roberta C. Bondi,
Professor of Church History at Emory University of Atlanta, Georgia

As we've already seen, creative ideas for communication can be stimulated by Bible stories and by our own stories. This third category is a "catch-all", and includes material inspired by:

The lives of friends
The lives of acquaintances
The lives people we've read about
The lives of famous people
The "lives" of fictional characters.

There's so much material in Other Peoples' Stories. The challenge is to heighten our awareness of the stories that we're hearing and observing. Once we've become alerted to this, the task is to decide how best to portray the story so that it will honour the person it has been inspired by and communicate something worthwhile.

It should be said that if we're going to react to events and people around us, then the themes of the ideas we come up with will inevitably be quite random. We're unlikely to discover a poem or story or idea which exactly fits the specific brief we're working on at the time. We have to receive the ideas as they happen, whether or not they fit neatly into the current creative project. It may be that later we'll find an outlet for them, or maybe not.

The difficulty is that most of us are influenced by the goal-oriented society which we live in, a society in which time is of the essence and efficiency is all that matters. This pulls us toward the unhelpful habit of only producing ideas which are practical or useful. In such a culture, when are we allowed to create for no apparent reason? Surely we create because that's how we're made, not because we can use the ideas for some practical end. But this is not always how it works in practice.

It's so important to free ourselves from the strait-jacket of only ever creating for a given theme. It's not just an issue of whether or not we work well under pressure. Working to a brief almost inevitably means that the ideas are steered toward what we need them to say. This means that they are held back from taking on a life of their own and developing in a direction that wasn't anticipated when you first put pen to paper (see *The Flowers Told On Me* monologue earlier, page 64). Thus we miss out on one of the most exhilarating aspects of creativity — to see an idea coming alive and virtually writing itself.

One way of dealing with this difficulty is to turn the pressure of deadlines and specific briefs on its head. By using a notebook to build up a reservoir of ideas which "just happened" and weren't driven by the need to produce specific projects, we allow ourselves to become more proactive in the themes and ideas that are being considered. More than that, we move on in the process of finding our voice and expressing the ideas that we're wrestling with at the time. But if we believe that everything must have a use, then having a store of previously unattached ideas also means that when we need a particular idea, it's quite possible that we've already got something scribbled down in one of our notebooks which could be lifted and adapted. This helps in two ways:

1 It takes the pressure off when you have to produce ideas for a specific brief
2 It also provides more incentive to play with ideas that occur, since you know that one day they might flourish into something useful.

As you'll see, on this path of the journey I've been challenged to move away from only being able to create caricature characters (who were mere ciphers for what I wanted to say) towards being able to portray increasingly real and rounded people with whom others can identify and empathise. Of course, some stories suit caricature characters, but it's good to have a range.

The next piece takes us back to 1989 (when, you'll remember, all things had to be explained). It's a good example of a fairly two-dimensional character. But it's a light idea, so that's appropriate enough.

I'm A Skoda
(1989)

(Written to be performed in a strong Lancashire accent)

I'm a Skoda, and I know it, 'cos most folks la' at me
A Skoda's life, it ain't such fun.
They think if they collect enough shell tokens, I come free
A Skoda's lot is not an 'appy one.

I'm a Skoda, and I know it, 'cos I don't fit in
A Skoda's life, it ain't such fun.
They reckon I'm the very first four wheeled biscuit tin
A Skoda's lot is not an 'appy one.

I'm a Skoda, and I know it, 'cos I'm being overtook
A Skoda's life, it ain't such fun.
They go right fast them push bikes, it's embarrassing to look
A Skoda's lot is not an 'appy one.

I'm a Skoda, and I know it, and it's true I'm nothing grand
A Skoda's life, it ain't such fun.
I cannot go right fast, 'cos they've not oiled me 'lastic band
A Skoda's lot is not an 'appy one.

I'm a Skoda and I know it, and me rust has gone too far
A Skoda's life, it ain't such fun.
But though it's right I'm rusting, it don't mean I'm not a car.
A Skoda's lot is not an 'appy one.

I'm a Skoda with a difference, I'm human just like you.
A loser's life, it ain't such fun.
Just 'cos I'm slow and ugly, you treat me like a Skoda too
A loser's lot is not an 'appy one.

❏	**Principle:**	Jokes are performable.
❏	**Springboard:**	Which jokes have you heard which are both funny and say something? How would you adapt such a joke into a different format?

I'm sure you've spotted the starting point for this poem was the series of Skoda jokes going around at the time. Back in our days of messing around in youth group sketches we'd worked out (rather cleverly) that sketches had punch-lines, and so did jokes. So we applied our razor-sharp logic and began to act out jokes. But there was also a serious side beginning to come through.

In An Hour

(1990)

(The following statistics are from the year 1990 and they happen in our country in the space of one hour)

In an hour we make a fifth of a double decker bus
And the tax man takes four million from us.
In an hour one million goes to charity
And double that to VAT.

In an hour half a Porsche gets on the road
But more than half the price is probably owed.
In an hour we're all another hour old
And the OAPs are feeling cold.

In an hour — a hundred tonnes of chocolate sold
And the zit attack is taking its hold.
But in an hour we can afford to grin
We've grown a hundred square metres of brand new skin.

In an hour there are three accused of rape
We spend a hundred grand trying to change our shape
We spend the same amount on changing our hair
And over a million on what we wear.

In an hour — six Girl Guides retire
One person is the victim of a serious fire
In an hour we smoke twelve million fags
Spend seven hundred grand on books and mags.

Make half a million pounds worth of British cars
And spend the same amount on beer in bars.
Save six hundred grand for a rainy day
And much the same amount is gambled away.

Five million people talking on the phone
But no official figures for those without a home
Hundred people join the dole
We buy two hundred grand's worth of toilet roll.

Seventeen marriages join them down the pan
Man blames woman, woman blames man.
That's thirty-four people now divorcée
A third on the grounds of adultery.

Five hundred *Mayfair*s leave the shelf
Thirty-one abortions on the National health
Two more people amputees
And a hundred unwanted pregnancies.

In an hour seventy-three meet their final hour
Seventy-three meet their final hour
Seventy-three meet their final hour.

And here we are
With God's great power
Living in an ivory tower.

(Or in an evangelistic context)

And here we are
With God's great power
Wondering why lives turn sour.

☐	**Principle:**	Facts can create huge impact when presented creatively.
☐	**Springboard:**	What facts have you always wanted to present? How could you present these facts to create an impact?

A friend of mine had a book listing hundreds of things that happen in Britain in one hour. The moment I saw it I knew there was a poem there. So I borrowed it and spent hours mechanically compiling and fitting rhymes together. As I said earlier: "One per cent inspiration, ninety-nine per cent perspiration." But I had hours of fun playing with it. Thinking back, I should've added a line like: "In an hour you can write about a tenth of a poem like this."

Writing *In An Hour* was largely a detached exercise. But the next poem was far from that — it just had to be written. I was beside myself with grief at the death of a friend, and for his widow he'd left behind. I didn't know how to pray for her. This was the best way I could find.

How Do I Pray?
(September 1992)

Lord, take every thought that remembers her,
Sculpt them in marble,
And let her stroll through the gallery
Entitled "Prayers for Cathy."
And let the artists let her
Let them be
Just what she wants them to be.

Wrap every wish that's wished for her
In bows and shiny paper,
And forward her to Christmas Day.
And keep her in that moment
When she realises they're all for her.
Then, let them be
Just what she's always wanted.

Collect every tear
That is shed for her,
And turn each into tiny mementos
Of past proofs of your power.
Then tattoo them on the inside of each eyelid.
That, on every blink
Her subconscious will soak in the subliminal
That you've always been just what she wanted.

Save every sigh,
That escapes for her,
Weave them into silk
Then stitch them with threads of hope
Into cross-shaped curtains for the windows of her eyes.
And hang them over the round window
The square window

The arched window
That, whichever window is today's window
Tomorrow's window
For ever's window,
She'll see them all through the frame that you hung.

Tot up every word
That is scribbled for her,
Times them by her telephone number
(the London one, it's longer)
Triple it
Add ten
Then turn each into angels
On guard for her heart.
And may you be the number one
She'll first think of.
And let no one ever take anything away
From her final answer.

⌐	**Principle:**	Pray for people by using your creativity.
⌐	**Springboard:**	Do you always pray spontaneously?
		Have you ever searched for the right words to express your hopes for someone?

Initially I just poured these gut reactions out into my notebook. The next day I attempted to tidy them up into a more coherent structure. This rewriting was not primarily about improving a poem, it was more about honouring the prayer that was at its core. Again, at the time it was very much a private event. It was not until three months later that, nervously and after much thought, I posted her a copy of the poem. She said it helped, I don't know how much. But I know it helped me to find a way of praying for her at the time, and hopefully this prayer joined with many others to help pull her through those first difficult months. At the other end of the spectrum, it wasn't all serious stuff.

Musicians Cheat!
(November 1992)

If seven tones
And five half tones
And, maybe, four lengths of tones

Can tot up to so many tunes
Then how many poems are out there waiting?

We have slightly more than a dozen words to juggle
You've just got to get the right words
The round right way

Anyway. Musicians cheat
They often use often the same tone more than tone once once:
"Do Do Do
So"
Wouldn't work in a poem, would it?

> ❏ **Principle:** It doesn't have to be heavy. Mess about more.
> ❏ **Springboard:** What profound thoughts have you had?
> Would they work as poems?

Mr Kalashnikov
(March 1993)

Mr Kalashnikov had a bright idea
55 million guns ago.

Today Mr Kalashnikov gets away from the hustle and bustle
Of every day rifle fire by going on quiet walks in the forest.
And he grows flowers,
You know, the things families put on the graves of loved ones.
And he's set up a fund to help the victims of "bright idea"
He had 55 million guns ago.

Mr Kalashnikov is now 73,
And still living with it.

> ❏ **Principle:** Imagine yourself into the mind of a famous person.
> ❏ **Springboard:** Who else's mind would you wonder yourself into?
> Do you ever wonder how certain famous
> people might feel?

Ideas rarely come from the same place twice. This was sparked by an article in a Sunday magazine about the man who invented the infamous gun. But I don't now search through Sunday papers when I want to write a poem. Ideas just happen, and we just need to become better at recognising them when they do.

God Is...
(November 1993)

They say he's a pie in the sky,
A grey beard, a reason to die, the one to be feared,
A rubber stamp, a cage
A genie's lamp, a wage
They say he's a magic wand, a bad wager
A being beyond a sergeant major
A map, they say he's a mop
They say he's a happy clap or a pill to pop
A prop, they call him a crutch
A crop, they think he's a soft touch
A safeguard, a shining knight
A membership card, an invite
A vacuum, a facade
An empty room, a cheap charade
A flag to fly, a fog
A fag, they say he's a lapdog
A peat bog, a punch bag
A long slog, a dreadful drag
A dragon, they say he's a drug
They say he's a band wagon, a bug
Or even a bugging device
A booming voice, a terrible vice, a last choice
A lucky charm, a slippery slope
A strange calm, a last hope
A holy glow, a cut throat
A way to go, a scapegoat
A cheap dope, the one to blame
For the can't cope, a Sunday game
A raging sea, a green mist
A policy, an iron fist
A fake, they think he's a spying eye
A piece of steak, a pie in the sky
(Repeat from beginning)

(At different pace, as a reflection on the above, possibly while the above
poem continues)
They say it's a guessing game
That goes round and round
They say he hides his face to tease us
But personally I've found...
He's like Jesus.

	Principle:	A brainstormed list can be transformed by finding the right structure.
	Springboard:	What list of attitudes, reactions and excuses would you love to express?
		What other structure would help you do this?

It would be nice to be able to say that I spent days on the street doing a straw poll on people's views of God, but I can't. Even so, I would imagine that a lot of people would be able to put their tick next to a number of these impressions of God, saying: "Yes, I'd agree with that."

The idea came when I was reading a book. The author made a short comment about how different people see God in different ways. He only gave about four examples, but it sparked something in me. I spent hours coming up with a whole range of possibilities and putting them together in a simple structure to make a poem. Later I thought: "What's my reaction to all this? How would I answer these people?" I knew, in today's climate, people might not react well to a dogmatic answer in absolute terms, but to simply add my view to the list would be allowed. Hence the end lines.

Happy Families
(December 1993)

Narrator	Once upon a time there was a right time to tell a story from ancient folklore. That time is now, so... Once upon a time in a far away land there was a family, a father, a mother and a son. But it was more than once upon a time that this family argued. And each time they argued all three were convinced they were right and no one would give in to the other two. Once upon one of these times the father said:
Father	We should go and talk to Gwayling.

Narrator	...who was a wise old man from another land.
Father	He would sort this out.
Narrator	The other two wanted to say what a stupid idea this was, but they couldn't, because it wasn't, because he would — sort this out. So to cut a short story slightly shorter still, they all trooped off to see Gwayling — the wise old man of the village.
	As each explained their relative grievances, Gwayling sat there motionless and serene — he'd actually fallen asleep, but once they'd woken him, he managed to bluff:
Gwayling	So you're not getting on then?
Narrator	He wasn't called the wise old man for nothing (in fact they had to pay him a lot of money, but that's another story). He gestured enigmatically for them to follow him. He took them down several flights of stairs, through a series of heavy, dusty doors and into a large room, where a table was laid with the most sumptuous looking food they had ever seen.
Son	Well even if we don't solve the argument, at least we get to pig out!
Narrator	...said the son.
	Gwayling drew himself up to his full five foot two and a half when he stood on the curb, and launched into his big speech:
Gwayling	All food must be eaten before you can leave the room.
Son	What a blow!
Narrator	...said the son, reaching forward to grab a prawn cracker.
Gwayling	Wait! I haven't finished yet.
Narrator	He wasn't used to being interrupted.
Gwayling	All food must enter mouth while still touching chopsticks — otherwise that food will turn to stone.
Father	No such thing as a free lunch.
Narrator	...said the father.
Mother	No such thing as invisible chopsticks...
Narrator	...said the mother.
Mother	Who laid this table?
Gwayling	I was getting to that! Don't you people ever stop interrupting?

Narrator	The old man went to the cupboard and when he returned with the chopsticks they all realised something was terribly wrong. The chopsticks were a metre long, two centimetres thick and had none of the fancy coloured writing you normally get on chopsticks — they could only be described as broom handles, primarily because they were broom handles.
Son	These are broom handles!
Gwayling	Well spotted.
Narrator	He was surprised at how quickly he was picking up the sarcasm. He got back to his "setting the challenge" speech while he was still on a roll.
Gwayling	All food must be eaten before you can leave room. All food must enter mouth while still touching chopsticks — otherwise that food will turn to stone.
Narrator	And he added with a certain flair:
Gwayling	Enjoy your meal.
Mother	But this is impossible. Our arms aren't long enough.
Gwayling	Which is why there is a riddle written on each napkin folded skilfully around the chopsticks.
Father	Why is there always a riddle in these stories?
Narrator	The father had always been terrible at crosswords and was beginning to feel a touch threatened, but he knew his folklore pretty well and asked:
Father	Shouldn't there also be one last clue that turns out to be the key that neatly solves the riddles?
Gwayling	Yes, but I must say it as I close the door ominously behind me.
Father	Fine.
Gwayling	(Closing the door) Try it one at a time.
Narrator	He made the turning of the key as sinister as he could — which was very — they really had got to him.
Narrator	The father said:
Father	Stupid idea to come and see the old codger in the first place.
Narrator	...and for once they all agreed.
Mother	Well, let's read out the riddles.
Narrator	...said the mother, taking control.
Father	Mmmmm
Narrator	...said the father, losing it.
Narrator	They all undid their skilfully folded napkins and read

the riddles simultaneously.

Father You heard the man, the one last clue that turns out to be the key that neatly solves all the riddles was: "Try it one at a time".

Narrator So the father read his:

Father Maybe get by our.

Narrator The son read his:

Son We'd more not own.

Narrator And the mother read hers:

Mother All food feeding faces.

Narrator They all sighed a hungry sort of sigh and the mother said:

Mother Well I don't get any of them.

Son Nor me

Narrator ...said the son.

Father Phew!

Narrator ...said the father.

Son Maybe the old slaphead is a demented psycho cannibal bent on eating our hunger-weakened bodies while he laughs at the meaningless riddles that become our dying words.

Narrator ...said the son, cheerily.

Father Maybe you've been watching too much children's telly.

Mother Maybe we should just try and eat.

Narrator So they did. They tried different approaches; different angles; different grips; different styles; but no matter how much they contorted their bodies they couldn't get the food into their mouths while still touching the chopsticks. Then it dawned on them — they'd been there all night and now the sun was rising — and the dawn made them realise just how hungry there were. So they went back to their riddles.

Mother Try it one at a time.

Narrator ...repeated the mother

Son Try what one at a time?

Father Try what one at a time?

Narrator They stood there repeating "Try what one at a time?" until the audience made the connection... (waits for audience) ...maybe not. The father leapt up and

	shouted:
Father	I've got it! The words, the words of the riddles, one at a time, try the words of the riddles one at a time.
Narrator	And they did. The father said his first word:
Father	Maybe...
Narrator	Then the mother:
Mother	All...
Narrator	Then the son:
Son	We'd...
Narrator	Then the father said his second word:
Father	Get...
Narrator	And the mother:
Mother	Food...
Narrator	And the son:
Son	More...
Narrator	And:
Father	By...
Mother	Feeding...
Son	Not...
Father	Our...
Mother	Faces...
Son	Own! Maybe all we'd get food more by feeding not our faces own! Yes that's sussed it, much clearer now Dad!
Narrator	But the father knew he was onto something:
Father	Try it the other way round, you go second.
Father	Maybe...
Son	We'd...
Mother	All...
Father	Get...
Son	More...
Mother	Food...
Father	By...
Son	Not...
Mother	Feeding...
Father	Our...
Son	Own...
Mother	Faces.
Father	Yes! Maybe we'd all get more food by not feeding our own faces. Bring me a crossword quick!
Narrator	And they all realised this was it; the one last clue had

turned out to be the key that neatly solved the riddles — and yet they seemed surprised! So each began to feed the other in turn: the father fed the son, the son fed the mother and the mother fed the father, then just because they could they swapped the order round and then they just randomly fed each other just for the joy and fulfilment of serving each other. On tasting the last morsel they left their erstwhile prison and returned to tell their friends of the wonderful lesson they'd been taught by Gwayling, the wise old man from another land. In time, the story was passed down from generation to generation, which is why today the saying "Maybe we'd all get more food by not feeding our own faces" is as well known as other sayings like "Looking after number one" and "God helps those who help themselves".

Don't you just love a happy ending? Well tough! Real world! Truth is, they never got out to tell their tale. Gwayling, as I said, wasn't called a wise old man for nothing: he locked the door, threw away the key, sold their house and their possessions and blew the money on a luxury world tour eating, each evening, in some of the best restaurants in the world. Which is probably why no one today seems to have heard of the saying "Maybe we'd all get more food by not feeding our own faces".

Maybe once upon a time to come.

	Principle:	Adapt a known story to your style.
	Springboard:	What stories do you remember from childhood? How would you tell them now?

We don't have to create brand new stories. There's a wealth of old stories waiting to be rediscovered, stories with roots in the traditions of the verbal storytelling which was such a central part of society in the past. Recently this type of storytelling has enjoyed a renaissance — people telling old stories, adapting them, adding to them, telling them in their own voice. This last story is my adaptation of an old story; the riddle bit is lifted from an old idea (in an old notebook) and inserted into an established story.

It often happens that when ideas occur they have no obvious use at the time, but often (providing they are stored) they come back to you when you're looking for something specific. It's a great moment when you find yourself thinking: "So that's where that goes!" Finding a proper home for an idea you've put up in temporary lodgings is very fulfilling. But the reverse is also true — that it's so frustrating to find the perfect home for an idea you had, but not be able to locate it because you left it wandering with no fixed abode.

Addicted
(December 1993)

I never thought I'd get addicted. Most of my mates were doing it. I never thought it could get so out of control. At first it was just a bit of fun — I know it sounds stupid but it was — doing homework was fun. I never thought I'd get addicted. The first time I did some — what a buzz! I felt so grown up. But it soon wore off, and I couldn't wait 'til the next time I could do some. Then we started taking stuff to parties. We'd sneak off to the bedroom and start doing some there.

At first we'd each bring our own, but after a while we started to swap and share biros and that — we knew it was dangerous; what with the risks of different handwriting and the chance of getting caught, but that was all part of the buzz. I was getting marks I hadn't got before. My mates had noticed too, and it felt good! It made me stand out — obviously I hid the marks from my parents, but my mates looked up to me for it , or I thought they did. Slowly I became more and more isolated from them, but I didn't mind — it gave me more time to do my own stuff.

The only problem was that now there was no buzz. I was doing more and more, but it was leaving me cold. This was the start of the Cravings. At the end of a lesson I'd start twitching and shivering. What if they wouldn't give us any more? It was the start of the shakes. By this stage I'd started experimenting with making my own stuff. At first it was just mixing different subjects — but fairly soon even that didn't get to me. I needed more. Other kids would pass me their stuff, but I'd shoot through it and still need more. So I started to steal. At first it was only small stuff like sneaking into classrooms lunch time and copying down essay titles from the blackboards. But it wasn't long 'til I was breaking into fifth-form lockers and taking chemistry assignments.

Then the big boys got to hear about me: somehow they find out that you're hooked so they started pushing their stuff on you. And they make you pay through the nose for it — not just money either. They don't care about you, they just give you the hard stuff. Stuff you're not ready for. Stuff you can't handle — and yet at the same time the very stuff you're craving for. You know you're out of your depth but there's nothing you can do about it.

This is when you start hitting the low grade stuff. It's the shakes, you lose concentration, you can't focus, you start to make a hash of the whole thing. And that's dangerous, because the big boys don't like to be messed with. You get all the bad side effects like black eyes, headaches, dead legs, so it's even harder to concentrate, you make mistakes, you get careless, you lose your grip. Then the teachers notice, they call you in , they spot the tell-tale signs; the bleary eyes, the coffee stained jeans, the black ink round the mouth and the fingers. Then they asks you to empty your pockets and you know the game's up. You pull out the chewed pen-tops and the stolen essay titles asking you to compare and contrast the different types of heroine in mediaeval French literature.

It all started so innocently. I never thought I'd get addicted.

❏	**Principle:**	Take an established setting (drug abuse) and insert an unexpected ingredient (homework).
❏	**Springboard:**	What other unexpected ingredient could you insert into this structure? What other structure could you use?

That sketch and the next two were produced in response to specific commissions. This is a different discipline to writing whatever the muse dictates at the time, and one where the principles laid out toward the end of the section on *How Can We Be More Creative?* can be helpful.

Saying "No" To Drugs
(December 1993)

(Family sitting around the dinner table eating their evening meal. If this never happens in your family — imagine it!)

Mum	What did you do in school today, Martin?
Martin	(Mumbling) Oh nothing...
Mum	Don't mumble Martin.
Martin	(Over the top) Oh, *nothing!*
Mum	You must have done something.
Martin	Well, we had this bunch of guys in talking about drugs and that.
Mum	Drugs and what?
Martin	Well drugs and... you know.
Mum	I'm sorry but I don't. What did they say?
Martin	Oh just the usual stuff about saying "No" to drugs
Dad	(Looking up for the first time, quite forcefully) We don't want any child of ours saying "No" to drugs
Martin	What?
Dad	We don't want any child of ours saying "No" to drugs, do we dear?
Mum	Certainly not darling. No son of mine is going to be caught saying "No" to drugs.
Martin	But drugs can be dangerous.
Dad	Martin, we know the dangers... (to mum) ...don't we dear?
Mum	Absolutely, your father has spent a lot of time looking into this: the addictive tendencies, the side effects, the destruction of brain cells, the petty crime often associated with an uncontrolled drugs habit, the risks of HIV and AIDS and of course, heaven forbid, the sore throat and runny nose. We do understand the dangers, Martin. Your father's done a wonderful job.
Dad	Why, thank you dear.
Mum	Well you have, darling. You've been very thorough.
Martin	And yet you still don't want me to say "No" to drugs?
Dad & Mum	(Together) Absolutely.
Martin	What?
Mum	You mean "Pardon?" Martin.
Martin	Yes... No... I mean "Why?"
Dad & Mum	(Together) Well, it's...
Dad	Sorry dear, after you.
Mum	No, that's fine, you go on.
Dad	No really, I interrupted you.
Mum	No, no, you were already talking.

Martin	(Interrupting them) Is it because you want to allow me to make my own mistakes?
Mum	Goodness no. Not if we can help it.
Martin	Is it because you want me to take responsibility for my own life?
Dad	Yes of course we do. But we don't...
Martin	Or is it because you drink and smoke, so you think it would be hypocritical of you to stop me taking other drugs?
Mum	That really is quite rude of you, isn't it darling?
Dad	Absolutely. Yes, we have a glass of wine with our meal, and yes, we smoke socially, but that's not the same.
Mum	Well actually dear, I meant the fact that he interrupted you in mid-sentence was rude.
Dad	Yes, it was, wasn't it.
Martin	And you never do that do you dad?
Mum	Don't be so sarc...
Dad	(Interrupting) Of course I don't.
Martin	Well, is it because you did drugs when you were my age, so you don't feel you've got the right to clamp down?
Dad & Mum	(Together, strongly) How dare you!
Mum	Sorry darling, do go on.
Dad	Thank you. (Strongly) How dare you! That's very impertinent of you. Isn't it dear?
Mum	Absolutely. Do we look like ageing hippies?
Martin	Well...
Mum	Don't interrupt. How dare you accuse us of taking drugs, however long ago.
Martin	Well why don't you want me to say "No" to drugs, I just don't understand. Don't you care?
Dad	Of course we care, and if you hadn't butted in quite so often we would have told you why.
Martin	(Genuinely) I'm sorry. Forgive me.
Mum	At last, some proper manners.
Dad	We don't want you to say "No" to drugs because, well... would you like to tell him dear.
Mum	May I? Thank you. We don't want you to say "No" to drugs because in these days of declining manners, and general rudeness, we're not having you letting

us down in front of other people. We absolutely
insist that when you are offered drugs, you're very
clear in saying "No, thank you".

Dad	Now do you understand?
Martin	(Still unsure) Yes.
Mum	Yes, what?
Martin	Yes please.

| ❏ | **Principle:** | Start with the punch-line and work back. |
| ❏ | **Springboard:** | Take a punch-line you know and create a scene from it. Take any line, at random, from a book and use it as a start or end line of a story, sketch or poem. |

This idea is just an extension of a classroom joke:

| Teacher | "Yes, what? |
| Pupil | "Yes, please." |

Or:

| Teacher | "No, what?" |
| Pupil | "No, thank you." |

Again, many of the ideas that become written pieces have been
bouncing around our brains for years. Bringing them forward into the
conscious mind is easier once we understand some of the principles.

Compassion Fatigue
(March 1994)

(The doctor must be very low energy throughout, until specified. In
contrast, the patient must provide considerable energy, and would
generally talk at a much faster pace than the doctor. This is necessary
both for the character and to maintain the pace of the sketch.)

Doctor	(At desk, reading medical notes of patient) Do sit.
Patient	I'd rather stand, thanks. (Begins to pace the room)
Doctor	Any better?
Patient	(A little frantic) Not at all Doctor.
Doctor	Mmm.
Patient	And it's getting worse. I'm sure I've got it.
Doctor	Mmm.
Patient	I'll be fine one minute, then suddenly it attacks.
Doctor	Same things?

Patient	Yes.
Doctor	Starving African children?
Patient	Yes.
Doctor	War-torn countries?
Patient	(Worried that an attack may start) Don't!
Doctor	The Band-Aid song?
Patient	Especially the Band-Aid song.
Doctor	Mmm, pretty standard.
Patient	But now it's not just the news, or charity begging letters: there's no telling when it'll strike — from walking past the homeless in town to watching that really gaunt weather girl on the BBC; the same symptoms.
Doctor	Lethargy?
Patient	Yes.
Doctor	Indifference?
Patient	Yes.
Doctor	Coming over all apathetic?
Patient	All those.
Doctor	(Even more apathetically) Mmm.
Patient	(Particularly high energy level) My energy suddenly gets drained. The muscle fatigue I could live with but it's a complete mental and emotional exhaustion. I'm getting really worried about it Doctor. You've got to help me this time. I've definitely got it, and it's getting worse — last weekend it came on in church!
Doctor	(Showing the first hint of interest) In church?
Patient	Yes.
Doctor	Mmm. That is unusual.
Patient	I've got responsibilities you know. There are things I could be doing, but I'm laid up half the day with these attacks.
Doctor	I know, but I told you. I can't cure it.
Patient	Why not?
Doctor	(Matter of fact) Because you haven't got it.
Patient	How do you know? (Getting a little riled) You haven't even taken any blood tests so how can you know?
Doctor	I know you haven't got it.
Patient	How?
Doctor	Because I have! I know what it's like, I know how totally debilitating it is. And look at you; strutting up

and down the surgery like some hyperactive cockerel. You exhaust me just looking at you.

Patient Look, I didn't know you had it as well. And OK, maybe mine's not fully developed yet, but at least give me some drugs to hold it back.

Doctor (Even lower energy than before) There are no drugs. I've tried them all. There is no getting better.

Patient (Shocked) I didn't realise.

Doctor No one ever does, they assume we can't catch it. They assume we can see all these ill people all day and be immune from it. Well we can't. I'm proof.

Patient Look, I had no idea. I'm sorry.

Doctor (Sarcastic) Oh great help!

Patient Couldn't they give you a month off or something. Just 'til it's under control?

Doctor A month off for something that doesn't exist? It's not a "proper disease", not according to the NHS. To them, I'm just shamming. "Lethargy", "apathy", they're not tangible symptoms. So I'm just told to "snap out of it".

Patient I know.

Doctor No you don't.

Patient OK I'm sorry. Is there anything I can do? Can't someone talk to your partners, try to explain.

Doctor Wouldn't help.

Patient Well we've got to go higher then. I'll write to the NHS or my MP or something.

Doctor What's the point? Accepted medical knowledge says there's no such thing.

Patient There must be some study on this, enough people have got it. Hasn't anyone done any research?

Doctor Don't know. Haven't looked. Probably wouldn't get funding for it anyway.

Patient (Getting an idea, and suddenly even higher energy) But if you got funding, would you do research into it?

Doctor (Shrugging shoulders) Might. But where do I get that sort of money?

Patient I've got my contacts. Can you knock together an account of the disease for me; basic symptoms, maybe some case studies, all you've got on it; and I'll

	make sure the right people get to hear. I'll crack this.
Doctor	Will you?
Patient	It's the least I can do. I'll be in touch... Oh and thanks. I haven't felt this good for months. I knew you'd cure it. (About to leave)
Doctor	You didn't have it.
Patient	OK, maybe I didn't.
Doctor	You did something: you came to see a doctor. So you couldn't have it. If you really had it, you wouldn't care that you had it, 'cos it knocks out your response system. So you can't help yourself or anyone else. The victims sit in their sofas and watch it slowly eat away at their energy, their feelings, their ability to care. But they don't care — that's why it's called "Compassion Fatigue" (Stares into middle distance, then snaps back into flippancy) Not that I care!
Patient	So how do you cure them then?
Doctor	We don't. But then that's not my problem is it?
Patient	(Beginning to understand) Because you don't care.
Doctor	Right.
Patient	Because you can't.
Doctor	Exactly.
Patient	Yet. That's where I come in. I'll speak to you soon.
Doctor	Apparently.
Patient	(Leaving with a sprightly walk) Thanks again.
Doctor	Yeah, sure. (Suddenly lively once he's left) And he thought he had Compassion Fatigue! I haven't had such sympathy since I fell off the Death slide at Pontins. And so quick! Normally, I've got to lay it on really thick — at least ten minutes worth of total lethargy to get the first inkling of any concern. I hate the deception, but it gets results. Works every time!

Principle:	Take a known expression (compassion fatigue) and make it literal.
Springboard:	How else could you make compassion fatigue a literal disease?
	What other expressions could be literalised in this way?

The idea for the following sketch happened when I was watching television. No prizes for guessing which programme.

Death By Soap
(May 1995)

Powder	G'day Michael.
Producer	Why g'day Powder. Great performance on yesterday's shooting by the way.
Powder	Thanks Michael. You've met Buck, my agent, haven't you?
Producer	Yeah, g'day Buck.
Agent	G'day Michael.
Powder	We were wondering if we could have a little chat, Michael?
Producer	Why course you can Powder. (Hammed up) Hey look, here's a sofa, why don't we all sit on the sofa and have a chat. (They sit)
Producer	Now, is this "little chat" as "Good guy, chum, general mate" or as "Producer of highly successful soap: *Flying Young Doctors Home in the Country Practising Away on Neighbours*"? I just need to know which hat I'm wearing here.
Powder	No, as "Producer of highly successful soap: *Flying Young Doctors Home in the Country Practising Away on Neighbours*".
Producer	Right. (Puts different hat on)
Powder	I never did explain metaphor to you did I?
Producer	(Confused) Mmm?
Agent	Listen Michael, Powder's very grateful to *Flying Young Doctors Home in the Country Practising Away on Neighbours.*
Powder	Right. I'm grateful for all the work it's given me.
Agent	And she's grateful that Powder Minose is now a household name.
Powder	But I'm feeling restricted Michael.
Agent	It's not a challenge anymore.
Producer	Would you like your script later? Less time to learn it?
Powder	Not that sort of challenge Michael.
Agent	We're talking about "artistic challenge".
Producer	Heck, no wonder I didn't spot it.
Powder	It's just that I could do so much more.
Producer	Right. You want to make pop records.
Powder	No.

Agent	Well yes, maybe.
Powder	Yes, maybe I could make pop records as well, but I know I've got some serious acting roles in me too.
Producer	We could make *Flying Young Doctors Home in the Country Practising Away on Neighbours* serious.
Agent	You're joking, right?
Producer	No, I'm serious.
Agent	Exactly. It doesn't work.
Producer	Right.
Powder	I feel hemmed in Michael. There's more to acting than being in a soap. I want to be able to engage my emotions, I want to be believable, I want to deal with real life. Develop a career I can be proud of, a career that'll stretch me, that'll give me the chance to meet my potential.
Producer	Sorry, drifted away there Powder, you couldn't keep your sentences down to a couple of lines could you? Concentration span and all that.
Powder	Look Michael you've been a real mate to me, but (Producer goes to swap hats) no that one's fine, but with due respect...
Agent	Yeah, with due respect.
Powder	*Flying Young Doctors Home in the Country Practising Away on Neighbours* is like chewing gum.
Producer	Sorry?
Agent	It's like wallpaper.
Producer	Sorry, is that metaphor again?
Agent	Well, strictly it's simile.
Producer	Good, as long as it's close.
Powder	It's not even good quality wallpaper. It's wood chip.
Agent	It's wood chip put up by workmen with grubby fingers.
Powder	Badly.
Agent	With overlaps and visible air pockets.
Producer	(Confused) So what are you saying?
Powder	It's just not me anymore.
Producer	Right. Fine. As long as you're sure.
Powder	I'm sure.
Agent	She's sure.
Producer	Right. (Calls his secretary on intercom.) Sheila, could you call in Bruce, Chan and Susie for me. (To Powder

and Agent) It'll take some rewriting of course, these sort of big plot changes take quite a lot of messing about with. It has to build, it has to dovetail, it has to merge with all the other subplots and character developments the guys are working on at the moment, but they're quick writers so I reckon by about... oh... three programmes' time we'll have that wallpaper changed for you.

Powder	Michael, I want to leave the programme!
Producer	For grief's sake Powder, I said I'd change it. What do you want? Look, whatever colours, whatever patterns, you've got it.
Agent	She feels there's a new life ahead of her.
Powder	New challenges.
Agent	New horizons.
Powder	New possibilities.
Agent	There's more out there, Michael.
Powder	And I want to go for it.
Producer	Oh right, you just want to leave the programme.
Powder	That's what I've been saying.
Producer	Well, heck Powder, why don't you just come out and say it. (Bruce, Chan and Susie arrive)
Susie	G'day Michael, this better be good, the ideas were really buzzing in there.
Producer	Guys, this is big stuff. You have to find a way of killing off Powder. She wants to leave the programme.
Agent	Ah. When you say "Kill off..."
Producer	They can make it tasteful.
Agent	No it's not that.
Producer	Or dramatic.
Agent	No it's not that. It's just that it's a tough world out there. Does she have to actually die?
Producer	I don't know. (To the writing team) What do you think guys?
Bruce	Well maybe you...
Susie	You mean "she".
Bruce	Sorry, she. I get real life and what happens outside the programme mixed up sometimes, but maybe she could, uh... I don't know...
Chan	Be lost in a boating accident?

Bruce	Nah, been done.
Susie	Maybe she could...
Chan	Move to Adelaide to be a student?
Bruce	Nah, been done.
Susie	Move to New York to follow a modelling career?
Bruce	Nah, been done.
Chan	Be in a car accident and end up in a coma?
Susie	'Cos then we could just shoot the hospital scenes.
Bruce	Nah, been done.
Chan	It needn't even be her if she's covered in bandages.
Bruce	Nah, been done.
Susie	There must be a way she doesn't actually have to die.
Bruce	I've got an idea. Maybe she doesn't have to die. Maybe her character is played by a different actress and... nah.
Susie, Chan & Bruce	(Together) Been done.
Bruce	I don't see any way round it. She has to die.
Chan	All right, "die" but if things don't work out, maybe her dying was all a dream, all a terrible dream.
Bruce	Nah, been done.
Chan	Really?!
Bruce	I know. Good one eh?
Susie	Unbelievable...
Chan	I've got it. Your idea about her character being played by a different actress, right. Well, her character has some plastic surgery done...
Susie	To look like the new actress, yes?
Chan	Right. Then later she decides she doesn't like it, and she wants to look like she did before...
Susie	So she has the plastic surgery reversed...
Chan	But because it's not an easy operation she actually turns out looking a little bit older than she used to...
Susie	A year or two, however long it's been that she's been out of the programme...
Chan	So it's perfect for her to step back into the part if her new career doesn't take off.
Producer	Right, let me think that through.
Agent	'Cos there's no guarantee she'll make it.
Powder	It's all about getting the right breaks really.
Agent	Being in the right place at the right time.

Powder	'Cos it's not what you know but who you know isn't it.
Agent	And even if she does make it for a while you never know when you might hit a bad patch.
Powder	So if there's a way I don't actually have to die...
Producer	Oh right, so that's what this is all about, is it?
Agent, Powder, Bruce, Susie & Chan	(Together) Yes.
Producer	Sorry, I didn't spot that little "plot development". So what do you think guys? Does she have to die, or what?
Chan	We could try the plastic surgery idea?
Producer	No, it's a bit too complex. I'm not sure people would follow it. Sorry Powder, but you have to die. Anyway Powder, do you want this "new life" or not?
Powder	Well yes.
Producer	I mean, do you really want to go for it, or just stay safe?
Powder	Well...
Producer	Do you really want to find the "real you", or just keep your options open?
Powder	Well...
Producer	Do you want to give it all you've got, or keep on looking over your shoulder all the time? Do you want to dive in, or just dip your toe in the water? Do you want to make a leap of faith or keep holding onto the railings? Do you want to stay on the tree or fall to the ground, die, then grow into a new tree in your own right?
Powder	Michael.
Producer	What?
Powder	You're using metaphor!
Producer	Heck, I am aren't I!
Powder	You're right. I have to die.
Producer	And maybe I could be a writer!

❏ **Principle:**	Use identification with someone else's story as a parallel to an issue you want to deal with.
❏ **Springboard:**	What other TV characters could you satirise? What if you put TV characters from different programmes together in one sketch?

The next three pieces are all inspired by the struggles of a particular friend. As with the *How Do I Pray?* poem earlier, these were my attempts at getting in touch with his struggles and in a sense praying for him in them. Again, they pretty much wrote themselves.

I've Got A Friend
(July 1995)

I've got a friend who doesn't exist.
I talk with him a lot,
And he talks back.
But I know he doesn't exist.
He told me he's spent his whole life not existing.

Which is handy,
Because when you don't exist you can't spoil anything
When you don't exist you can't harm anyone
When you don't exist you can't harm yourself
Although you can try your best.
And he's convinced he doesn't exist.

But the more I believe in him
The more I'm sure he does.
The other day he told me he thought he had low self esteem.
We jumped around the room!
We both knew
That to have a low self esteem
Means you must exist.

❏	**Principle:**	Real life conversations provide starting points for ideas.
❏	**Springboard:**	What anecdotes or stories do you tell which could be adapted into poem or story or sketch form?

As you can probably tell, this conversation actually happened. It's just one of those that somehow becomes more real by writing it down. If you've read the book *Mister God, this is Anna* you'll know that when she found something important, she got her friend to "WRITE IT DOWN BIG." It seems that the act of committing something to paper (or computer screen) cements it in our mind. This is especially true when you don't just record what happened (as you might with a diary), but you stay with the idea long enough to

find a way of expressing its significance more fully. You've honoured
the moment by giving it time. You've filed it under "I" for Important
Moments.

More Than An Orphan
(July 1995)

How does the fatherless son hear his father's going to die?
How does a father, already dead, die?
After years of relief at not having to say the first two words of the
Lord's Prayer,
After years of wincing when someone wants to sing "Abba Father".

How does the orphan not hate himself
When he hears his heart hope it'll be painful?

How does the more-than-an-orphan not hurt himself
When he his hate-hardened heart wrings its hands and relishes
revenge?

How does the more-than-an-orphan hope for good things
For the soul of the one he knew had no soul?

How does the more-than-an-orphan dare to hold at last
And be held at last by the dad who died three decades past?

How does the more-than-an-orphan hear his father
Finally find the words:
"I love you and I'm so pleased with you"?

God knows.

⌐	**Principle:**	Questions can be more powerful than statements.
⌐	**Springboard:**	Have you wondered how people you know cope with their pain? How would you attempt to express your wonderings?

Again, this was in response to an actual situation. This was me trying
to understand how my friend could respond to news of such
dimensions. The final line was a short, but very significant prayer.
The line about the Lord's Prayer also got me going on another tack.

Our Father
(July 1995)

Our Father
Or mother
Or other phrase
For those whose childhood phase
Knew no better days.

Whose art is in heaven
And whose gallery graces the globe.

Hallowed
Not shallowed
Be thy name

Thy kingdom come
And may we wait awake.
Thy will be done
And may we give it weight and worth
On earth
As it is in heaven

And give us this day
For we don't doubt
Each dawn is born of you.
So too, our daily bread.
And, as we dare to utter:
"And a little butter too?"
The great I AM, is making jam!

And forgive us all our trespasses
Our forward passes
Our buck passes
As we forgive those that pose
As nettles in rose petals.

And we plead:
Lead us not into temptation
But deliver us a double dose of righteousness
To rout the evil.

For thine is the kingdom
That counts,
The power
That mounts the attack,
And the glory
That must go back
To you.
For ever and ever.
Amen. Again. Amen.

| ❏ | **Principle:** | Take a well-known passage, meditate on it. Then reword it until it's fresh again for you. |
| ❏ | **Springboard:** | What other well-known passages have lost their impact for you? How would you reword them? |

There's a rich seam of material to be found by entering into the struggles of friends. But that's *not* why we stand with them in their troubles: "No, I'm not really concerned, but keep talking — I can feel a great poem coming on." Obviously not. But I've found that writing has been one way I've managed to connect with their struggle, be with them through it, and pray for them to progress out of it. The big question is… do you let the person read it?

You have to use a considerable amount of wisdom to know what to do. Sharing the piece with the person who unknowingly inspired it could be really helpful to them, or could be really invasive. You have to know them well, and they have to know that you love them. We're told, if we need wisdom, we should ask God for it. Whatever you decide, it's important to consider how they might react if they were to read it. By considering how they might react, you will be more inclined to honour their struggle by making it as true as you can.

Related to this is the use of stories in helping people see where they're out of line in some way. The way the prophet Nathan dealt with King David after David's sin with Bathsheba (2 Samuel 12) is a wonderful example of the use of creativity in getting through to people. God told Nathan the prophet to go and confront King David with what he'd done. What a job! David had committed adultery with Bathsheba and had her husband killed to cover it up. David must have known he was well out of line, but there was no way he was about to admit it. David's defences were stronger than any Philistine barricade. What was Nathan to do?

Maybe Nathan weighed up different approaches. Should he try the softly, softly approach? Or the strong confrontational "Thus saith the Lord..." approach? Neither seemed exactly promising! Then he had the idea of telling David a story. He spun him a tale about a poor man who had his pet sheep stolen by a rich land baron who had plenty of sheep of his own. David's sense of injustice was engaged and he reacted from his gut: "He should die for doing this! Who is this bully?" Nathan told him "You are the man", and David knew it was true. He was broken. God had got through, and was then able to begin the process of bringing him back.

Observe the situation, pray, prepare the story, show or tell the story, and then see how they react and whether they see themselves in it. It can prove a most effective way of getting people to see themselves and their actions in a new light, without necessarily having to point the finger. Sometimes a little exaggeration helps:

Lord, Take Control
(Sepetember 1997)

Lord, take control of my life.

Lord, take control of my life right now.

Lord, I insist that that you take control of my life right now.

Not only do I insist that you take control of my life right now but I demand that you make me feel as if you've taken control of my life.

And Lord, I reserve the right to complain and moan about you to other people if, at any point, I sense that you've not taken control of my life.

And just for you to know (because I've asked you to do this before, and frankly you've not made a very good job of it have you?) I will continue to carry on exactly the way I am until you prove to me that you can do a lot better at taking control of my life when I tell you to.

Because if you don't take control of my life, then somebody has to...

Lord.

Amen.

❏	**Principle:**	Exaggeration can help us see ourselves as we really are.
❏	**Springboard:**	What tendencies have you observed in others (or yourself) that you could exaggerate to make a point?
		What would you do if they didn't see themselves in it?

It's good to be able to laugh at ourselves!

Paradise Crushed
(November 1997)

This was a full forty-five minute piece of physical theatre which I was commissioned to write for the Baptist Missionary Society. They wanted some drama to illustrate the issues facing Third World countries. The aim was to motivate Christian people to be more active in their response to the situations their missionaries are working with. Having studied Third World development issues in my economics degree, I'd always felt very strongly about these issues. I'd often wondered whether I'd ever get the chance to put something together about how the First World has disadvantaged the rest of the world by the way we trade with them.

The thought process that led to *Paradise Crushed* illustrates the journey I've made through this book. My initial reaction on receiving the commission was to adapt a piece I'd written in December 1992, which was essentially an anger-riddled rant on injustice. It was a full-blast, in-your-face attack on people's apathy towards the evils of world trading structures. I thought it was really powerful and rammed the point home so powerfully that people would have to do something. On reflection, it was probably just me getting a buzz from triggering people's guilt glands. I'm sure now it merely served to activate their defence mechanisms and did little to motivate any response. Don't read all of this, you'll get the idea pretty soon...

Justice, He Knows How It Goes
(December 1992)

Understand how underhand
Is the way we trade
And the money made
From the Third World
From the hand of the poor
Where the Third World war
Is paid for
By the blood and sweat
Of the ones in debt.
And there is no doubt, the money mounts
'Cos by all accounts their account's over due.
They've been fleeced by the few

And the fleece wet through with the morning dew
And all because they looked for a sign
And the sign said:
"Buy now, pay then."
Or was that "pay them"?
And them, and them, and them and them and them, and then
Them as well, 'cos they lent to them, who were advised by
Them, and marketed by them, and they all need their cut,
Their commission, their slice, which is nice, 'cos they
Didn't do much, 'cept be born at the right place, the right
Time:
The West.
Now.
It's not what you know, but who
That counts the amounts that you earn for your firm.
"Firm." Mmm. Apt.
Or maybe "Rigid" would be better.
"Solid", "stiff", "tight", "vice-like",
With a voice like hell
When the bell tolls
For your debt to be paid.
And the IMF pin stripes types, in the shade
At their dolling out parade.
Tutting, as they're gutting,
And they talk about upping
The austerity programme
Or they "simply won't lend any more."
Promise?
But the war doesn't stop
When they drop to their knees
And beg for a freeze
From the men with degrees
And they're told, so cold
"You've still got to meet your commitments."
And they drown in tears
As fear leers
And lashes in their face
With its tongue
And the only way is down
From the bottom rung
Of the ladder laced

Each rung greased
With the drippings from the feast
Of the top ten per cent
Who rent,
At reasonable rates,
The rest of the world to its owners.
We run a global pawn shop
For the pawns
Too poor
To barricade their door from the West
Living like kings in our castles
Keeping well down all the dirty rascals
Who probably like being poor.
Less stress.
And "more is less"
Well, more or less
But with less than nowt
There's less of a shout
In the life stakes
As Death takes
His task to the limit.
No mask
From the minute they're born
They stare in his face
And death doesn't blink
Death doesn't blink
Death doesn't blink
What d'you think;
Is it really our fault?
When demand and supply
Spits in the eye
Of the needled
The needy.
And the greedy gripe
About the type
Of butter on their bread
"I can't believe it's not better."

But we spread it on thick
And it makes us sick
And we fix their price

By a roll of a dice.
Which is nice
'Cos it's loaded
With care.
With adults there
And not a sharp pointed scissors in sight.
And not a thought for the Third World's plead
As they bleed.
'Cos we're blind to the world's injustice
Malpractice
The Judas' kiss of our Third World trade.
We're afraid
'Cos some say:
"The time ticks on
'Til the time bomb blows
And the anger grows
And the Third World
Pay back what's owed."
We sold so much
In our soul sale
But we're out of touch
With the size and the scale
With the rise of the gale in the south
And some say:
"Don't freeze, this breeze
Will fan into flame
Old Guy Fawkes' game
And the fireworks fly in the eye of the West
And the gain we got
Again and again
Will be forgot
And won't remain."
So some say
So some say
And be that as it may
But he'd say:
On the day when justice reigns
He'll take our gains
From our greedy games
And call to account
The amount

That was ripped off
Tipped off
Stripped off the stride of the poor
He'll call "no more"
To the ones who
Say their grace
Then chase the pace
That trails a trace of blood to the bath
To the blood bath
On whose behalf?
— Our own.
And whose is the blood that's shown?
Those
Out there
Alone they dare to groan "unfair"
Their prayer
Goes home
To the One
Who'll own their care
To the throne
Of Justice.
'Cos Justice
He knows
How it goes
When innocent blood flows.
He knows
How innocent blood flows
He knows
He knows.

❏	**Principle:**	Just because you get a buzz from doing it doesn't mean it connects with the audience.
❏	**Springboard:**	What issues do you feel strongly about?
		How would you like to communicate them?
		How would it work best to communicate them?

Mmm, that really warmed people, didn't it?! Now they're really going to want to do something about it, aren't they?! And for all the right reasons!! (Yes, and sarcasm works really well written down, doesn't it?)

The fact that it's all true doesn't mean that people will take it to their hearts and do something about it. I cringe now at the memory of the one and only time I performed this. Five years later I've realised that people react more positively when allowed to empathise with people's stories, than when they're shouted at. I'd also learned, from personal experience, that people are more likely to be spurred into action when inspired rather than cajoled. A new angle was needed...

I set about telling the story of a fictional family, shipwrecked on an idyllic island and living in a self-sufficient community. All was fine on this island until the day the helicopter came. The helicopter men persuaded the people that they could help develop their island. So trees were cleared, sugar was planted and a bumper yield was harvested. But the sugar crop had flourished worldwide and the price of sugar had plummeted — so they didn't have the coins to buy the food they needed, or the new seeds for next season, or the money to pay back the loan for the machines. Gratefully they borrowed more money from the helicopter men. The winter floods came and since the trees had gone, the floods washed the soil into the sea, so the next year's crop failed. Then interest rates went up and their loans were even harder to pay back. So the cycle continued, and they had to learn new words like "poor" and "debt" and "TB".

The gradual unfolding of one family's story draws the audience into empathising with their plight. When their daughter Ellena develops TB the audience feel genuine compassion. The irony is that these fictional characters become more real than the pictures of starving African children on the TV, because we've learned to defend ourselves against them. So when the audience are encouraged at the end of the show to suggest ideas about what we can do to help Ellena (and all the other Ellenas), they want to do so, because they care. Further, because they've proposed the ideas themselves, they are far more likely to put them into action than if they were told what they should do by someone with a harsh voice and pointing finger.

Conclusion

I'm convinced that this approach of telling stories and asking questions is both more respectful and more effective than trying to cajole people into action. If motivation by coercion works at all, it generally produces action fuelled by guilt. In contrast, people who have chosen to act produce a far more wholesome dynamism. Tom Houston (President of World Vision) quotes the following story about communication styles:

There is an old fable about a contest between the sun and the wind to see who could get a man to take off his coat. The wind blew harder and harder, and the man only drew his coat closer around him. Then the sun sent out its warmth, and in a short time the man willingly took off his coat.

Which would we rather be? The wind or the sun? We'll pick up on this theme in the final section of the book. But before that, I'll leave you with some more of the questions that God's been asking me along this part of the journey:

Are you getting through?
Will you enter into other peoples' pain?
Do you tell other peoples' stories to make them look good?
To make you look good?
Or to make me look good?
Have their stories affected you before you tell them?
Do you feel you have to shout at people to motivate them?
Do you believe that they are made in my image?
Do you believe that they want to do good, if they knew how?
Do you trust me to inspire them to action?
Can you inspire them to action without me?
How do I talk to you?
When do I talk firmly with you?
When do I inspire and encourage you?
Which do I do the most — talk firmly or inspire?
Will you be more like me?
Will you tell more stories?
Will you ask more questions?

The View From This Point Of The Journey

The View From This Point Of The Journey

You may remember from the introductory chapters how we used the Six Questions of Craft (Where? Who? What? When? How? and Why?) to develop thoughts and give structure to creative ideas. Now we'll use the same questions as a structure to draw together the thoughts and challenges of the journey so far. By asking these questions we can move toward some answers on the core question of "Are We Getting Through?"

1. Where do we communicate?
— On common ground.

While preparing this book I came across a study book called *What do you mean "communication"?* written by Nicki Stanton (published by Macmillan). A central point of the book was that of finding common ground on which to communicate:

> Gaining attention through motivation or the use of need satisfaction, is a far stronger method of gaining co-operation than through such devices as fear-arousal, coercion or exhortation, and so on. Success [in communication] depends on finding out what a person's needs are and choosing the most appropriate appeal. Information is most readily received if it is
> a   relevant to the audience's needs and interests;
> b   confirms the views and attitudes already held.

Applying this to an outreach context, we would have little problem with her first point. It's understood that we need to be relevant to the audience; to deal with issues they're interested in; to answer questions they're asking. But the second point is slightly more difficult. How can the Gospel "confirm... views already held" when they evidently don't agree with the Gospel? How can we have common ground with people who don't agree with us? This question is even more difficult as we read on, and grudgingly admit that she's right:

Two significant findings illustrate this. Firstly, party political broadcasts: people tend to watch the broadcast of the party they support and switch off the broadcasts of other parties. Second, advertising: research into the response of readers to advertisements shows that we are more likely to read thoroughly an advertisement for something we have already bought. In both cases, we find the views expressed are comforting because they confirm our original beliefs and attitudes.

So how is it possible to persuade people about something they currently don't believe in, while "confirming the beliefs and attitudes they already have"? How can we find common ground with these people? By considering who it is that we are trying to communicate with...

2. Who are we communicating with?
— Fellow fallen image-bearers.

The crucial question that any communicator must ask is "Who am I communicating with?" The answer? — people exactly like us. Christians and non-Christians have huge areas of common ground, attitudes on which we would wholeheartedly agree. This is because we're all made in God's image. No matter how far we've fallen from God's plan for our lives, we all still have a remnant of God's image in us. In our communication we can aim to appeal directly to the central core of God-given humanity that people retain, despite all that would seek to destroy it. Dr Larry Crabb in his book *Understanding People* (Marshall Pickering, 1988) states:

> My starting point as I try to understand people is this: people are fallen image-bearers. I accept this premise because the Bible accepts it.

This belief is central to our faith. It is also a key to the communication of our faith. This is how we gain, and hold, peoples' attention long enough to be heard. This is non-confrontational outreach. This is common ground.

Nicki Stanton would tell us that if we start with the things we disagree on ("You are sinners and you need to change your lifestyles") then people won't "watch our broadcasts or read our advertisements" — however Right we are. But if we begin with the things we do agree on, if we focus on the values that are central to us being human, then we're far more likely to get through.

Once we have something of a relationship because we have views in common, they might trust us enough to ask us about the views we have which differ from theirs. This then becomes genuine communication. It has graduated from being one directional (us telling them what they should believe) to a two-way voluntary exchange of ideas. Nicki Stanton writes:

> Communication is a selfless process in which, to stand any chance of success, we have to fight constantly our natural instinct to be self-centred. We have to guard against our very natural inclination to concentrate on ourselves, on what we want to say, and try instead to consider the other person and focus on what we need to say and do, both to help them understand what we mean and to help them tell us what they mean.

Real communication, then, is a two-way process. We must be prepared to listen as much as speak and we must listen effectively to what is really being said — and to what is not being said.

Obviously, this principle applies to personal witnessing, but it is also relevant for those of us who communicate "from the front". The crucial ingredient in creating common ground is the desire to work with, rather than against the people we are trying to reach. This will happen naturally if, like Larry Crabb, we see people as fellow fallen image-bearers. But we'll struggle if we see people primarily as fallen and forget that they are also image-bearers, as Calvin clearly did:

> ...Whatever is in man, from intellect to will, from the soul to the flesh, is all defiled and crammed with concupiscence [perverted self-love].

If this is our view of the people we're aiming to communicate with, this will inevitably affect how we relate to them. It comes back to the story Tom Houston tells about the sun and the wind (see page 152).

A balanced belief in people as fellow fallen image-bearers frees us to become less like the wind and more like the sun in our communication. We won't have to fight with people, or shout to make ourselves heard. Rather, people will be happy to engage with us and listen to our ideas.

3. What should we use to communicate?
— *Stories.*

Stories are a natural vehicle for putting this approach into action. As I've already quoted, C.S. Lewis says: "We read to know we're not alone."

Stories create empathy and identification — common ground. Stories can also appeal to the remnant of God's image in people; if we show them characters they aspire to; characters which inspire the better side of their characters; if we give them stories which remind them of what they genuinely think and feel about life's important issues; if we go one stage further and honour their humanity by asking for their reactions to these stories — then we are creating common ground from which we can genuinely communicate.

> Without fighting, stories have won over more people than all the great wars put together.
>
> Ben Okri, *Birds of Heaven*

> Whenever stories are told, stillness falls. We cease our restless frittering. During these times of concentrated devotion to alternative realms we may reconnect with the power of creation we may rest momentarily. Through such resting we are renewed. Renewal inspires the courage to change.
>
> Alida Gersie, *Earthtales*

Which is exactly what Jesus did!

Jesus' communication:

> A salesman had a machine to sell. This machine had completely changed his life and so he wanted everyone to have one. He'd learnt all the specifications, had trained himself in its every function and could answer any question on its workings. The only problem was: no one ever seemed to ask him any questions, and although he made a point of telling them anyway, they didn't seem to listen. Some actually told him he was boring, others took offence and told him not to be so pushy, but most just made excuses and walked away. He didn't want to be pushy, he certainly didn't want to be boring, he was just excited about the machine, but what could he do? After much heart searching he decided to go back to the designer, who'd asked him to sell it in the first

place. He asked him how he would sell the machine to people today. It was fascinating to listen to him.

Or, as Gordon Bailey has put it:

> Three characters walked along the top of a high and narrow wall. The first one was Jesus, who was followed by Faith, who, in turn, was followed by Experience. So long as Faith kept his eyes on Jesus, Experience followed and they all made secure progress together. If Faith took his eyes off Jesus and looked to Experience, he fell off the wall.

How would Jesus communicate today? We don't know. All we have to go on is what he did when he was here. By choosing to use stories Jesus found common ground with his listeners. He used images and examples which people related to. Jesus knew exactly how "fallen" people were and yet he still honoured them by telling stories like the arable of the Good Samaritan — a story which not only answered the question "Who is my neighbour?" but also inspired people toward generosity and compassion. Jesus told stories which portrayed the kingdom of heaven and resonated with the humanity of those that heard.

> To poison a nation, poison its stories. A demoralised nation tells demoralised stories to itself. Beware of the story-tellers who are not fully conscious of the importance of their gifts, and who are irresponsible in the application of their art: they could unwittingly help along the psychic destruction of their people. A people are as healthy and confident as the stories they tell themselves. Sick story-tellers can make their nations sick. And sick nations make for sick story-tellers.
>
> Maybe there are only three kinds of stories: the stories we live, the stories we tell, and the higher stories that help our souls fly up toward the greater light.
>
> Ben Okri, *Birds of Heaven*

If we can emulate Jesus in telling stories that will not "poison our nation" or make our nation "sick", but will "help their souls fly up toward the greater light", then we counter the pull of the enemy on peoples' minds. We also create large areas of common ground from which we can communicate with people. We can inspire them to reconsider where these good values come from and encourage them to ask who this "greater light" is. On this ground they feel safe enough to look at the Source of their humanity and how best to enjoy life as it was meant to be lived.

Telling stories today:

Most would agree that Jesus was The Great Story Teller, but recently more people seem to have been following his example. Since the early 1980s there has been a gradual revival in the art of storytelling in Christian (and secular) circles. The Bible Society has recently recognised that the power of storytelling needs to be reclaimed by the church. They've set up a project called The Open Book which aims to help create and serve Christian storytellers.

Many of our leading communicators are increasingly using stories to connect with people. Listen to their thoughts:

> I have spent quite a lot of my Christian ministry in Bible teaching and especially apologetics, but it struck me some years ago that to convey a truth is not enough; we need to apply truth to people's lives to make it relevant to their situation. Jesus did this by using word pictures and stories which act as "windows on the soul" and which the Holy Spirit can use to make truth live.
>
> Rob Parsons, Executive Director of Care for the Family

> We in the West have been fairly good at stating and explaining the Gospel truth through theological propositions, sometimes even using logical or scientific processes to prove it. We are now beginning to realise what many of the Christians in the East have known all along — that major and important truths are also communicated through metaphor and allegory — in other words through storytelling.
>
> J John, speaker

> The use of story enables the speaker to paint a vivid and colourful portrait in the mind of the listener. If you throw a body of information at people they will switch off very quickly, whereas if you invite them to take a journey with you through a story then they find that their imagination has been provoked.
>
> Jeff Lucas, vice-president of the Evangelical Alliance

Conversion… is a collision of narratives. God's story touches my story and your story, and a collision takes place. People encounter stories that call their own stories into question, and they are forced to reconsider: What if my story isn't the whole story? How should I respond? In the process of reconsidering their own lives, they become caught up in the Story of Jesus, and they are changed.

Leighton Ford, former colleague of Billy Graham

Story is the way the majority of people learn their values. If you put a discussion about euthanasia on *Panorama* the vast majority turn off mentally, if not physically. But if you put it in the plot of *East Enders*, everybody's talking about it the next day.

Steve Chalke, Oasis Trust

4. When are we communicating?
— In a Post-modern era.

Steve Chalke's words brings us back to where we started this book: with the need to speak to people in a language they understand. As we've seen, our culture is changing around us. Post-modernism is changing the rules of the kind of approach people will, and won't, listen to.

This may well be one factor in the recent renaissance in traditional storytelling. People in today's Post-modern culture recoil from having absolute truth foisted upon them. The currency of today is much more "Does it work?" than "Is it true?" This philosophy has been perfectly captured in the title of the Manic Street Preachers' album *This is my truth, tell me yours*. Any claims we make to having absolute truth will cause many to put up their defences. Of course we know that their claim that "there is absolutely no absolute truth" may not be the most logical of assertions, but that doesn't help us communicate if they've already switched off.

Phil Wall is one of the many contemporary communicators who are aware of this:

The Gospel of Jesus is a story, the most amazing story ever told and relived day by day around the world. Just a cursory glance at the film and theatre industries shows us clearly that the redemption story is THE STORY being retold daily within these genres of expression. If our faith is to have any hope of communication in our increasingly Post-modern world the story of the Gospel and its inter-relatedness to our own story must once again come centre place.

Phil Wall, national evangelist with The Salvation Army

The journey I've shared with you in the *Writes Of Passage* began with the strong desire to communicate effectively; to speak in the right language; to "get through" to people. You've seen how this journey has repeatedly drawn me toward stories. Whatever the source of the idea (whether it's sprung from the Bible, or my own life, or someone else's life) I've been learning that the shortest distance between the truth and the human heart is a story.

Jesus faced a culture which saw religion as distant and legalistic. He had to communicate some very new ideas and he chose to use stories. Sadly, much of our culture today also thinks that religion is distant and legalistic. We can also use stories to intrigue people and draw them in to what "true religion" is really about. Let's allow God to inspire the creativity he's given us to tell stories of all styles and forms:

"You" stories
— Testimonies which say "Yes, my faith does work".
  Stories which satisfy peoples' search for reality, and get them asking questions.
  Stories which admit we have struggles, but that God is with us in them, and helps us through them.

True stories
— Stories of real people whose lives had been changed by The Story.
  Stories of friends.
  Stories of people you know.
  Stories of people you've read and heard about.

New stories
— Fictional stories which deal with the issues of today.
  Parables that carry hidden truth.
  New versions of old stories.

But how should we tell these stories?

5. How should we communicate?
— *As Jesus does.*

Let's look further into how Jesus communicated. Like all the best communicators, he changed his style according to who he was talking to. There were three distinct "voices" Jesus used to three separate groups. Mark makes it clear in his gospel that when Jesus spoke to the people he only used his storyteller voice: *"With similar parables Jesus spoke the word to them, as much as they could understand. He did not say anything to them without using a parable. But when he was alone with his disciples he explained everything"* (Mark 4:33, 34).

Matthew confirms this in his gospel: *"Jesus spoke all these things to the crowd in parables; he did not say anything to them without using a parable"* (Matthew 13:34). Both Mark and Matthew are pretty emphatic — Jesus spoke to the people in parables.

Jesus' second voice was that of the teacher. In Mark 4:34 he used this approach for his disciples, giving them clear, comprehensive explanation. Whether this was because they were slow to learn or hungry to learn is not clear, but in Mark 4:11 Jesus told them *"the secrets of the kingdom of God have been given to you"* in direct contrast to *"those on the outside"*, thus showing a deliberate, thought-through approach to give more direct teaching to those who were already part of the kingdom. This is why expository preaching is crucial, to teach believers the doctrines of our faith in a logical and rational way. Jesus also used some story and metaphor in the way he taught his disciples, but he also explained things clearly to them. But to the people who were still outside the kingdom, he only used parables.

Jesus' third voice was that of the confronter; reserved exclusively for the Pharisees and religious leaders, with whom he was pretty straight! In Matthew 23 Jesus speaks to the Pharisees in quite a different voice to the one he used with the people: *"Woe to you, teachers of the law and Pharisees, you hypocrites!... you blind guides... you white-washed tombs... you snakes, you brood of vipers."* Quite direct! But to the people he only spoke in parables.

So what are parables? I remember from my Sunday School days that parables are "earthly stories with a heavenly meaning." Stories which you had to think about if you wanted to learn about God. Often his parables were in direct response to a situation or a discussion that was going on. According to the context, he chose just the right amount of setting up (*"The kingdom of heaven is like..."*)

and packing down (*"...so will it be with you if..."*). So it was that those that were ready to hear would receive what God had for them next. It worked so beautifully:

- It was recognisable. He used images and objects from everyday life; sheep, coins, vineyards, which the people could easily identify with.
- It was attractive. We're told that *"the large crowd listened to him with delight"* (Mark 12:37). He obviously told the stories with great skill and charisma. He drew them in. The people were compelled by the truth of the human story and some dug deeper into the heavenly meaning.
- It was authoritative. Matthew says *"the crowds were amazed at his teaching, because he taught as one who had authority, and not as the teachers of the law"* (Matthew 7:28, 29). Who he was gave weight to what he said.
- It was intriguing. The whole approach encouraged people to think more deeply about the truths behind the human story and he was keen that *"those that have ears to hear"* would indeed hear.
- It was memorable. The use of vivid images locked the story in the mind of the listeners. The memory hooks were easy to recall, and so could be mulled over for a long time to come.
- It was honouring. Those that had no spiritual hunger weren't forced to consider issues they weren't ready for. Their free will was honoured and Jesus clearly had no desire to cajole people into thinking about the kingdom of heaven if they didn't want to.
- It was wise. Jesus knew that his charisma could easily manipulate people into following him. This could have led to converts who would turn out to be only fair weather followers. Jesus' whole calling was to bring good news to the poor (Isaiah 61), and yet he had the wisdom to do it in such a responsible way.

In a word, it was brilliant.

Some might say that Jesus was just fitting in with his culture: "They did that back then." This may be true. If stories were a common form of teaching in those days, then Jesus knew he had to talk to the people in language they could understand. But other sources indicate that religious teachers spoke in an academic and intellectual way, and that Jesus was unique in his approach. In which case he had the courage to stand out against the norm, and communicate in the way he knew would work. Either way, we're told that Jesus chose to talk to the people exclusively in parables, using images and ideas which people recognised and related to easily, stories that would intrigue them enough to consider the nature of the kingdom of heaven.

Others might say that Jesus was unique, and we shouldn't dare to copy him. Clearly he was unique in that he was fully God. But he was also as fully human as we are, since Jesus the man was also made in the image of the creative God. He was *"just as we are, yet without sin"* (Hebrews 4:15) and called, just as we are, to bring good news to the people. In John 14:6 he says *"I am the way, the truth and the life"* and later in verse 12 he says *"anyone who has faith in me will do what I have been doing. He will do even greater things than these because I am going to my father."* This verse has generally been interpreted in the context of miraculous signs, with the church waking up to the fact that God can act miraculously today. But might it also be applied to other areas? Might this also be a mandate for us to do as he did, to tell new and even greater parables? Will we use our God-given creativity to tell new parables?

Should we explain?

Throughout the chapter on ideas inspired by the Bible we considered the way in which Jesus didn't explain his parables; how he left them largely unexplained in order that those who had ears to hear, would hear. I've already shared some of my struggles on this — how in the past I've found it difficult to leave a story unexplained. Sometimes this has been because I've needed people to know that I've got something to say, sometimes this has been because I've not trusted God to speak without me helping him — telling the story and then going on to explain what I've already decided it means. By doing this I lose the essence of Jesus' approach: telling a story and leaving it with the people to consider.

But I'm learning. I believe that by driving it home we are in danger of stopping those who do have ears to hear from choosing to hear for themselves. Worse, we may even cause those who have not got ears to hear to be alienated by what they perceive to be over-forceful preaching.

Why is it so hard for us to learn? Why have we not thought: "If Jesus did it that way, and we're called to be like Jesus, then why don't we do the same?" Gordon Bailey tells this story:

> Having been invited to speak to a large number of young people, and having discovered that more than ninety per cent of them were wholly "unchurched", I spoke to them by means of a modern parable, which was filled with meaning but told without explanation. At the end of the story I said: "When you've worked out what I'm really talking about tell someone. Tell me afterwards if you wish." Members of the organising committee were verbally abusing me, accusing me of "throwing away an opportunity of preaching the Gospel", when our attention was drawn to a heated discussion going on outside, in which one not-yet-Christian young man was vehemently defending his perfectly correct understanding of the parable.
>
> Gordon Bailey, Schools Outreach Trust

Let me tell you a true story. Last September my wife Sandra and I were in the forest with her father, Manfred. It felt like something out of *The Lord Of The Rings* — it was dusk and the evening mist provided a stark contrast with the vivid green of the forest floor. Any second Gandalf could've walked out from behind a tree and uttered something profound! We were there to find wild mushrooms. Sandra had vivid childhood memories of being with her dad in the forest, searching for edible mushrooms and taking them home for her mum to cook. She promised me they tasted superb, and I believed her.

After half an hour only Manfred had been successful. He knew which ones were edible, where to find them and had already picked a hat full. Sandra and I had been wandering around, backs bent, searching intently but without finding a single mushroom. Each time either of us thought we'd found some, Sandra's dad smiled and shook his head — "Poisonous" he'd say, as disappointed as we were. But what could he do? If he pointed them out, then we wouldn't have found them for ourselves — we would've just picked them for him and somehow they wouldn't have quite been ours.

It was toward the end of our time in the forest that I realised what Manfred was doing. It suddenly dawned on me that the few mushrooms we had found had been close to where he'd been standing. The penny dropped. He'd seen them! He'd been standing there deliberately! He so wanted us to have the thrill of finding them for ourselves that he'd held back from pointing them out but just stood there and hoped we'd keep looking.

Believe me, they did taste superb, not least because we'd found them ourselves. If he'd not been the man he is, he might have got a real kick out of showing us how well he knew the forest and how good he was at finding the mushrooms. He might have pulled status on me, and made me feel like an ignorant city kid. He might have piled shame on Sandra, and made her feel guilty for forgetting "the ways of the country". But no. He understood the importance of us finding the mushrooms for ourselves and he loved us enough not to spoil the moment. What a superb teacher.

This event helps me understand a little of why Jesus left his parables unexplained. There can be no doubting Jesus' desire for people to learn about the kingdom, and yet he held back from explaining it all clearly. Intriguing. I need to learn that if I don't spell it out completely, those who really want to "find and taste the mushrooms" will keep looking. I need to learn the truth of the old proverb:

> Those that hear, forget.
> Those that see, remember.
> Those that do, understand.

A good story moves people from merely hearing (and possibly forgetting) to envisioning the story in their imaginations (and therefore remembering), and from there to doing something about it by engaging in reflection and/or discussion about its meaning (and therefore, potentially, understanding).

I need to learn to rely on the Holy Spirit to draw them into the thrill of finding the hidden meanings for themselves, understanding them and making them their own. I need to learn not to allow my enthusiasm for sharing these truths draw me into saying more than people are ready to understand.

I need to learn. Full stop.

Can we interact?

I've found one of the best ways of helping people to keep looking for the deeper meanings of a story is to ask them questions. By asking questions you can also guide people toward the answers you'd love them to find. As J John says:

> Jesus always seemed to be doing two things: asking questions
> and telling stories. Many Christians seem to be doing two
> other things: giving answers and "preaching".

By asking questions:

- You draw people in
- You create common ground
- You encourage interaction
- You honour who they are and the opinions they hold
- You encourage people that there are answers worth finding
- You indicate that you don't think you've got all the answers
- You affirm their right to choose whether or not to look for
  the answers
- You provide signposts, which help people toward finding
  the answers

The questions we ask need not always require answers. In some
contexts these questions are best kept rhetorical. You throw them out
only to provoke thought and to say: "Discuss" to the audience. But
in certain contexts it's also possible to enter into genuine discussion
off the back of a story. It may be that we need to take risks with the
way we structure events to allow for this. If we are going to ask for
response from people, it's crucial that the atmosphere and setting are
right, otherwise people will feel awkward and embarrassed. But if this
approach serves to engage people, and allows for effective
communication I think we'll be more than happy to alter some
structures.

A recent Grove booklet entitled *Preaching As Dialogue* looked at
the issue of giving people the opportunity to interact with the
preacher during the sermon, thus making the sermon a form of two
way communication. In this Jeremy Thomson says:

> The greatest preacher of them all asked questions, brought
> people into conversation took the observations and questions
> of others as opportunities to tackle the burning issues of life.
> Why have preachers forsaken him in this?

His arguments were fascinating, and showed that he had really grasped the principle of honouring peoples' free choice — a central part of how God has made us. He also clearly understood the importance of involving people. As someone once said to me "If you want to motivate somebody to do something, make them believe it's their own idea!"

With the recent changes this issue has become even more important. Today, people are more sensitive to being told what to think than fifty years ago. As Bob Mayo writes:

> In a pre-Christian culture Evangelism is not about explaining the Gospel but rather it becomes a process of telling and asking — telling the Gospel story and asking what they think... they work out the relevance of Christianity for themselves... the mistake... is to explain the story with a set of thoughts and ideas that do not mean anything to the person listening... Tell the story and shut up and listen to how the people react to what they've heard. There is no more simple method of evangelism than storytelling. It places the need for "personal discovery" and "working it out" (on the young people's behalf) alongside the need for "information transmission" (on our behalf).

> *Evangelism Among Pre-Christian Young People*
> (Ed Pete Ward)

Gordon Bailey says:

> It could be that many would-be communicators have become too dependent upon their own explanations instead of depending upon divine revelation.

Which brings us back to the thoughts of Nicki Stanton, with which we started this chapter:

> Real communication, then, is a two-way process. We must be prepared to listen as much as speak and we must listen effectively to what is really being said — and to what is not being said.

What's more, by telling stories and asking questions we give people the freedom to choose to think, consider and decide — that is, we treat people as we've been treated by our Father. As we learn how to do this we're becoming more like our Father.

6. Why should we tell stories and ask questions?
— *To give God space.*

When people are told what they should believe, there's nothing to discuss. The only issue is whether or not they accept what they're told to believe. But it's not just that people in our Post-modern culture may be put off by being told what to think. It's so much more than that:

By asking Where? we create common ground.
By asking Who? we treat people with respect.
By asking When? we learn the language of today's culture.
By asking What? we utilise the amazing power of stories.
By asking How? we use stories and ask questions, as Jesus did.

By doing all this we create an atmosphere in which genuine communication can occur. But more than this, so much more than this. Why? Because it makes space for God to speak.

- By telling stories and asking questions we relinquish control. We deliberately hand the story over to them and to God.
- By telling stories and asking questions we grow. We're stimulated to be creative in how we make and tell stories. Through this process we understand more about ourselves and God.
- By telling stories and asking questions we pray more. If God doesn't speak, it remains just a story.
- By telling stories and asking questions we become more dependent on God. Our stories will only change people's lives if God takes them to people's hearts.
- By telling stories and asking questions we stay humble. We have a clearer understanding that it's God's work, not ours.
- By telling stories and asking questions we give God the credit. We recognise that, ultimately, "getting through" is something only God can do.
- By telling stories and asking questions we're kept in awe. We hear of God saying things to people that we didn't even know were in the story.
- By telling stories and asking questions we grow in faith. We see God reaching depths in people we couldn't hope to get to, and we're encouraged to give the Holy Spirit even more space.

For it's…

Not by right, (nor by write) nor by repute
Not by clout, nor by cute
Not by colour, nor by drive
Not by thorough, nor by dive
Not by charm, nor by choice
Not by virile, nor by voice
Not by looks, nor by loud
Not by luck, nor by endowed
Not by favours, nor by fight
Not by brave, nor by bright
Not by polish, nor by gleam
Not by rule, nor by regime
Not by focus, nor by tact
Not by passion, nor by pact
Not by push, nor by press
Not by name, nor by address
Not by steal, nor by sword
Not by appeal, nor by applaud
Not by might, nor by power
But by my Spirit, says the Lord.

Who is God asking these questions to?

Are you getting through?
Are stories the language of today?
Do I want you to create stories?
Do I want to speak through your stories?
Will you develop the talents I've given you?
Will you start from where you are?
Will you play more?
Will you reflect more?
Will you fail more?
Will you persevere more?
Will you tell your stories?
Will you tell other peoples' stories?
Will you tell new stories?
Will you retell old stories?
Will you reach in more?
Will you reach up more?

Will you reach out more?
Will you be more you?
Will you use your own voice?
Will you ask more questions?
Will you listen more?
Will you give me more space?
Will you risk more?
Will you tell more stories
Will you trust me more?
Will you be more like Jesus?

If you sense God is asking you any of these questions, then use the remaining five Questions of Craft — Where? When? What? How? and Why? — to explore these issues further. May God inspire you to find the answers he wants you to find, as he continues to create in us a wonderful variety of versions of Jesus — who is, after all:

The *way* we walk
The *truth* we talk
And the *life* that enlivens both.

Epilogue

There was a land where most people didn't have ears to hear. No ears to hear anything that was said, sung or sounded. But a small group of people had miraculously been given ears to hear. These grateful people wanted to help those that couldn't hear. They tried to talk to them but, of course, they just couldn't hear.

So they came up with a brilliant scheme. They set up classes to teach the people with no ears to hear how to lip read. They thought, once they've learned to lip read, they can understand us when we enthuse about how brilliant it is to be able to hear, and maybe they'll want to hear too.

They advertised the lip reading classes and some people came. But most of them found it difficult to learn this new language and soon drifted away from the classes.

One day there was a crisis. The lip reading teacher was ill and unable to teach. While the committee were discussing what to do, a young man with a stutter offered to help. No one else wanted to step into the shoes of the master teacher, so they had no choice. It was agreed.

The young man with the stutter faced the people and then, to their surprise, he began to draw pictures. He drew a series of pictures that showed his story: how he'd come to be able to hear; how hearing had changed him; and how he'd never felt able to tell his story until he'd discovered that he could draw.

The people loved it, and understood it, and wanted to know about how they could hear.

But the committee were angry. They disciplined him, complaining that he was undermining the art of lip reading and showing no respect for his elders. They took away his pens and paper, and made him vow not to draw pictures again.

Eventually the Master Teacher recovered from his illness and returned to his task of educating the people who had no ear to hear. But they drifted away, as they had always done.

Other Resources Available

Live Performances
— *People Like Me*

With energy, comedy and disturbing honesty the performer moves through a series of characters and performance skills in his search for affirmation. One the audience have enjoyed the poetry, the mime, the juggling and the jokes they begin to recognise the "game", and become aware of the insecurity behind the skills. Slowly they are drawn into a touching autobiographical story, witnessing both the inevitable consequences of a life motivated by fear, and the possibilities it presents for those searching for self worth and unconditional love.

— *The Prodigal Grandson*

The Prodigal Grandson is an energetic and moving look at Jesus' wonderful story of the Prodigal Son. The characters from the story express their longing to be allowed to be "more than a five minute sketch", and to a new story unfolds portraying the next generation of the family. As in Jesus' original parable the human story is gripping and dramatic and has much to say about family relationships, adolescence and the search for freedom. But again, as in Jesus' story, the spiritual parallels are profound and challenging.

For the unchurched there is a glimpse of how God the father misses them and wants them to return "home". For church people there is the insight into the character of the elder brother, and what it may take for him to have a change of heart toward his brother. The performance concludes with a sense of God's joy at receiving his children back, and his pain for those who remain distant from him.

— *Paradise Crushed*

"All was fine on the island: the people worked, played and told their stories — until the day the helicopter came..." A spellbinding physical theatre show, telling the story of a Two-Thirds World family struggling for survival and dignity in the face of western attempts at "developing" their island. The focus of the show is on the role of the Christian faith in calling out "freedom" for the captives and binding up the broken-hearted (Isaiah 61 and Luke 4).

For information on bookings please write to the address below.

Cassette — *Prayers Poems and Parables*

The *Poems, Prayers and Parables* cassette was originally recorded and broadcast with Premier Christian Radio. It includes many of Rob Lacey's well-known performance pieces (such as *In An Hour*, *The Sower* and *The Prodigal Grandson*) and also includes some poems never before heard in public! Together they make up a collection of forty minutes of creative writing and performance designed to provoke thought and personal reflection.

Available at £6.00 plus 50 pence p&p

Video — *People Like Me*

The *People Like Me* show has been adapted for video to serve those who have enjoyed the show and may wish to see it again or introduce others to Rob's work. It can also be used as a discussion starter in small groups. The full show (recorded in live performance) has been divided into four sections with background chat from Rob and discussion questions laid out in computer graphics. We feel sure that you will find this a valuable resource.

Available at £12.00 plus £1.50 p&p

All cheques to be made payable to **R Lacey**
and sent to the address below:

Rob Lacey
101 Welham Rd
Streatham
London
SW16 6QH